PHILOSOPHY
FOR
AFRICA

Augustine Shutte

MARQUETTE
UNIVERSITY
PRESS

This book is dedicated to all those who help me be an African,
especially the people of St Mary's parish in Nyanga, Cape Town.

Thandanani nibe noxolo!

(*if we love there will be peace*)

David,

with warm good wishes

Augustine

July 2002

Copyright © Augustine Shutte
First Published in 1993 by UCT Press,
University of Cape Town (ISBN 0-7992-1487-6).
The financial assistance of the INTERPHIL programme of HSRC, for the research for
Philosophy for Africa, is gratefully acknowledged,

All rights reserved. No part of this publication may be
reproduced, stored in a retrieval system, or transmitted in any form or by any means,
electronic, mechanical, photocopying, recording or otherwise,
without prior permission of the publisher.

Typesetting and Cover Design by Karren Visser.
Cover photograph: *The Love Is Approaching But too much of anything is very dangerous.*
Linocut by John N Muafangejo. Copyright: John Muafangejo Trust, 1993.
License for Marquette University Press per Orde Levinson, Director,
John Muafangejo Trust, 1995.

ISBN 0-87462-608-0
Library of Congress Cataloguing-in-Publication Data
Shutte, Augustine, 1938-
Philosophy for Africa / Augustine Shutte.
   p.   cm. —— (Marquette Studies in Philosophy ; #5)
Includes bibliographical references and index.
ISBN 0-87462-608-0 (pbk.)
1. Philosophy, African. 2. Philosophy—South Africa.
3, Philosophy, Modern—20th century. I. Title. II. Series.
B5305.S5   1995
199' .6—dc20   95-41732

MARQUETTE STUDIES IN PHILOSOPHY NO. 5

MARQUETTE UNIVERSITY PRESS
MILWAUKEE

The Association of Jesuit University Presses

FOREWORD
for the American edition

South Africa is world-famous for apartheid—that unique racist philosophy and system constructed over the last fifty years. Because of apartheid (which means "separateness") another feature of South African life has been hidden from the world for all that time. But now the apartheid era has ended and our recent treasure has been revealed to the world by our president, Nelson Mandela, by public figures like Bishop Tutu and by events like the recent elections, the inauguration of the president, and the World Cup of Rugby. It is called UBUNTU (which means "humanity"). We feel it is something of great value we can offer to the rest of the world. This is what this book is about.

Philosophy for Africa was published in South Africa in 1993 and had a second printing in 1994. It seems likely that there will be a third printing in 1995. This is an indication of an interest that is surprising for a book of this kind. But it can be explained by what is going on in South Africa at the moment, and the relevance that the ideas discussed in *Philosophy for Africa* have in this context. Now that it is being published in the United States I want to take the opportunity to add something which will both highlight this relevance, and give American readers a more concrete vision of the context in which the book was written and is being read.

Philosophy for Africa is the philosophical engagement with traditional African culture of a South African brought up and educated in a European philosophical tradition, using the concepts and methods of this tradition. I was moved to this engagement because I had made the personal discovery of some ideas central to traditional African thought that seemed to me to be both importantly true and also able to make good a lack in our dominant contemporary culture and philosophy. I feel sure that the positive reaction to the book by South Africans from both European and African backgrounds is not so much because of its philosophical merit but because of the novelty of the intercultural engagement it embodies: African ideas analysed and critically evaluated by European philosophy. And perhaps not just because of the novelty, but also because we now perceive the necessity of this engagement at the deepest level, the level of vision and values.

This response to my book reinforced the truth of something that every South African has been forcibly taught by the *apartheid* system: the new South Africa will only be a viable human community if there is real integration at the cultural level. Different traditions of thought and feeling have to be integrated in every sphere—education, business, work, politics—if society and its institutions are to grow and flourish.

Integration does not entail uniformity, though a core of common values is necessary. But it does require familiarity and dialogue between different cultural traditions. In particular there is a need for critical and creative contact between the African and European traditions of understanding humanity itself, both as a reality and as a value.

This conviction, developed in conversation with kindred spirits, gave rise to the idea for a new project, which I call the UBUNTU project.

Central to my book is the conception of humanity embodied in the traditional African proverb *umuntu ngumuntu ngabantu* (a person is a person through persons). This understanding of human nature has its counterpart in the moral sphere in the idea of *ubuntu*. In English this is equivalent to humanity, understood as a moral notion referring to a general quality of character, of attitude or behaviour or way of life.

The notion of *ubuntu* is still alive in contemporary South Africa. It provides a natural focus for such contact between cultures. The aim of the UBUNTU project will be to investigate the different aspects of this conception of humanity, especially those concerning moral values, the virtues appropriate to different roles and positions in life, our social practices and political goals, the conception we have of human flourishing and fulfilment, and the meaning of human life and death.

The project will bring people together from different disciplines, academics as well as people from other walks of life (probably most of them African) who have personal acquaintance with the traditional background of the notion of UBUNTU, and who have studied or reflected on it in some or other way. One could envisage a poet or novelist, an educationist or a business-person, having something to offer, as well as philosophers, theologians, anthropologists and others.

The UBUNTU project will thus be formed about a nucleus of participants. Its identity and growth will be determined by the attempts of this community to understand and realise UBUNTU in the different circumstances which life in a new South Africa provides. Its first task will be to produce a publication reflecting the experience and understanding of UBUNTU that this nucleus has.

The aim of this publication would be systematic as well as comprehensive: to link the different aspects studied within a common conceptual framework, as well as to cover all aspects of real importance. It would also be practical as well as theoretical: to present the conception of UBUNTU in all its richness in such a way that its applicability to and importance for our present attempts to create a truly integrated and humane society would be clear. I would hope that it could make a difference to our business practice, our educational goals and methods, our treatment of prisoners, our evaluation of the different kinds of health-care professionals, our attitude to the police, to gender-relations—to the whole of our communal life.

What follows are my own reflections on some of the important issues that will need to be considered.

1. Human life, in whatever culture or society, is always animated and moved by visions of happiness or fulfilment and ideas of how these might be realised. This is in fact the religious dimension of human life. Every such vision and project of happiness includes a notion of the powers necessary and sufficient to realise it. Typically these powers transcend our own, either intrinsically or at least insofar as they lie under our normal ability to control. The gods are always seen as possessing power sufficient to achieve for us those things which we cannot but desire but which seem, for one reason or another, beyond our own unaided powers to gain for ourselves. Thus religion is that sphere of human life in which we seek, and perhaps find, the power to overcome even the most apparently insurmountable obstacles to a comprehensive and enduring happiness and fulfilment.

In a scientific and secular age it can seem that humanity is, in principle, in control of the world, with the ability to satisfy at least those desires we can rationally entertain. Increasingly however the evidence of the twentieth century points to a lack of control of our natural resources and an inability to satisfy humanity's material needs, in spite of technology sufficient for the task. The huge gap between the over-developed and the under-developed parts of the world is the ever-present sign of this.

Connected with humanity's apparent inability to control the forces of nature is a real inability to control itself. Opposition and conflict of all kinds and at every level prevent the kind of co-operation that could ensure the equitable distribution of the earth's resources and make it a home rather than a prison for the whole human family. Here if anywhere we seem to lack the power to change. If power transcending any under our control is needed for our fulfilment, it is needed here.

Clearly the power in question is not one that technology could supply; nor it seems could any political ideology and system. On the other hand in a secular age it is not possible to pin our hopes on supernatural powers or miracles. If power of a kind to realise human solidarity and creativity does exist, it will have to manifest itself differently in our time. This is the challenge that actual religions will have to face: they must find a way of empowering humanity to become a community (in every sphere of human life) and to make the world our common home.

Many religions are unable to do this, having not yet faced the challenge of secularisation. Other ideological systems born out of the secularisation process are unable to transcend it in any way, either theoretically or practically. They offer only a limited vision of human happiness, and are unable to achieve even what they offer. The question facing us is whether the religious dimension of UBUNTU has anything to offer in this context. How would its conception of the transcendent cope with secular culture? Is it able to find a way between a dualistic otherworldliness and the limitations of materialistic secularity? Has it anything to offer to our understanding of death and community with the dead? Is its attitude to ancestors simply part of a superseded sacral world-view which has no place in a scientific and technological culture? Can UBUNTU offer anything to facilitate dialogue between different religious faiths? These are some of the questions that arise out of a basic question about the religiosity of UBUNTU in relation to contemporary South Africa.

2. The view we have about human happiness is connected to our view of human nature, its needs, capacities and possibilities. The notion of UBUNTU surely has much to offer in this respect. In particular it would seem to embody a conception of human nature that avoids both the opposed extremes of materialism and dualism of contemporary European thought. Added to that is also an avoidance of both individualism and collectivism in its understanding of the relationship between persons and society. In spite of its insight into the radical dependence of persons on other persons to develop as persons, socialist and communist collectivist conceptions of society are rejected by UBUNTU as impersonal. Though completely dependent on society for all that they are and do, human individuals cannot be reduced to functions or roles within a mechanistic or organic whole. Human community transcends any sub-personal model; the best model is perhaps the family, a model which can be applied be-

yond the nuclear family to include a wider kinship system, even a whole people or nation, perhaps even the whole of humanity.

This emphasis on the interpersonal quality of humanity—embodied in the expression *umuntu ngumuntu ngabantu*—is at the heart of UBUNTU and the source of many of its distinctive insights and values. May it not well have something to offer to the reconstruction of a society formed by the spirit of apartheid? It may be that it can help us to avoid the bureaucracy and totalitarianism of all forms of socialism, as well as the inequalities and alienation inherent in liberalism.

Critical questions arise however? Can the emphasis on the personal and interpersonal really be maintained in a large-scale sophisticated society; is it not merely part of a pre-industrial village community? And what after all is a person according to UBUNTU ? Is freedom of choice, for instance, recognised—both as a fact and a value? How is it to be safeguarded in a communal society where interpersonal interdependence is so stressed?

3. Whatever the answer to these questions, this emphasis on the interpersonal character of UBUNTU is the source of many of the distinctive virtues or strengths of character recognised by UBUNTU . Lists of virtues name the ways in which human capacities are properly developed, the strengths of character that result, and the attitudes in which these find expression. UBUNTU has its own set of these; among them are patience, hospitality, loyalty, respect, conviviality, sociability, vitality, health, endurance, sympathy, magnificence. The animating spirit behind this list needs to be revealed. Surely it will have something to teach us about the moral life. It is important that virtues such as these—many of which are hardly recognised as such in contemporary South Africa—find appropriate expression in a developed world.

Consider, for instance, the virtue of respect, and in particular respect for the aged. Because of the dependence of persons on a personal milieu for their development as persons, personhood is a matter of degree in UBUNTU . It is also a task. Hence, other things being equal, an older person is more of a person than a younger one, with more to offer by way of personal influence and power. This means that the elderly should continue to play an important part in society, instead of being side-lined at the age of sixty-five. In the dominant European culture there is a cult of youthfulness that underlies many of our social practices from business to family life. To the irrationalities of these UBUNTU could well supply a corrective.

In general it could be claimed that the present tendency is to see morality as both merely conventional and largely private. It is difficult to see how one can establish a just society on this basis. UBUNTU certainly understands moral values as derived from our nature as persons and in this sense natural rather than conventional. And since personal life is essentially interpersonal, it cannot possibly be merely a private matter either.

Where European moral thinking tends to emphasise rights in the sphere of social ethics, UBUNTU gives duties pride of place. There are dangers in an exclusive use of either concept. Each derives from a different background; an understanding of these backgrounds could prevent such one-sidedness and make for a creative synthesis of the two moral insights.

4. There is the issue of nationality, nation-building, being a nation. It is certainly an unavoidable issue, and one to which UBUNTU has much to offer. The modern nation-state is an artificial and unworkable unit of humanity. It is both too big and too small. And it pretends to a spurious autonomy, that is merely a mask for self-interest and the inevitable cause of conflict. We must discover an alternative. The state is merely an institution to serve society. We must find other ways to identify the solidarity of people in a particular geographical setting. We must find another focus for our patriotism. Has UBUNTU anything in its store of traditional wisdom to offer us in this context? It is a context in which some principle of subsidiarity seems indicated, a way of integrating the local with the world-wide, the particular with the universal. Some things need to be centralised; some things cannot be. Loyalty is inherently locally rooted but there is no reason why it should not grow, extending its branches to embrace even a whole country. But for that to happen it needs to be fertilised by powerful ideas and watered by a spirit of solidarity. Can UBUNTU perhaps supply a spirit and ideas for this purpose?

5. Though it can only properly be the servant of a nation (or, more accurately, the instrument of a people), the state is nevertheless an essential institution in society. In that sense it is not artificial. But if government in all its aspects is to serve the good of persons, it must be organised and proceed in a humane way. Here too there is a need for subsidiarity. The basic unit of government should surely be the region, centred perhaps on one sizeable town. In that way a human scale is preserved. And officials can really know the people they serve and experience the effects of their policies. Perhaps the contrast between modern industrialised so-

ciety and the small-scale communities in which UBUNTU was conceived and grew up need not be so great after all.

Certainly UBUNTU would seem to have much to offer to both the theory and practice of government. First of all there is the virtue of respect for authority, something lost in the twentieth century because of its perversions. But good government without authority, and respect for it, is impossible. UBUNTU 's respect for authority may be open to abuse. There is the slavish following of leaders, the uncritical acceptance of custom and tradition, the inability to innovate. But there is also an understanding of the symbolic, rather than merely pragmatic, nature of all human authority. Authority, to deserve the name, is always exercised in the service of values that are rooted in humanity itself and have, as a result, an absolute character. It is these values which legitimate authority of whatever kind, rather than vice versa.

If government is to be the servant of the people there is a need for a more active involvement in the processes of government by ordinary people than has been the case. Huge bureaucracies are bad for humanity. Private and public sectors must be more closely connected, at both the local and the national level. UBUNTU embodies a tradition of consultation and decision-making that is very different from the centralised, from-the-top-down kind to which we have become accustomed. In the place of the idea of majority rule (which can sometimes mean a tyranny of the majority) there is the ideal of unanimity: "we talk until we agree". Though this might appear impossibly unrealistic, and certainly inefficient, it is in fact a formula for compromise. If solidarity is seen as an over-arching social goal, as society's proper product as it were, then achievement of agreement on the basis of committed dialogue is a value in itself, whatever the topic might be. Efficiency is not an absolute value; it is essentially an attribute of a means to an end. To be efficient about achieving an evil end is not a good thing at all.

6. Underlying styles of government are differing attitudes to reality and the possibility of knowing it. A common assumption is that in the realm of values, of moral and political decision making, there is no fact of the matter. In the light of this "truth by majority vote" appears a plausible maxim. What often happens in such a relativistic moral climate is rule by a combination of "experts" and "managers". The experts are the natural and human scientists: they give us the facts about the matter under debate. The managers then use this knowledge of the facts to implement the policies of the organisations, political or business, that they serve.

The policies themselves, the goals and values which influence everything else, simply reflect the interests of the powerful, the shareholders or the party.

UBUNTU recognises a form of knowledge that goes beyond science and is in fact the foundation for science. It is a kind of self-knowledge, and is best exemplified in our knowledge of other persons. Here objectivity is the fruit of authentic subjectivity rather than impersonal observation and measurement. It is a knowledge by involvement rather than abstraction. It is a necessary element even in the reasoned and responsible judgments of physical scientists. In the knowledge of human matters it is absolutely essential.

In our culture there is no question of rejecting or under-valuing scientific knowledge. But there has been a one-sided development that affects every aspect of our lives. The knowledge recognised by UBUNTU is its necessary complement and could restore the balance, not only in government and business, but in education and health care and many other fields as well.

7. Although it is opposed to the dominant forms of contemporary European thinking about human nature and society, UBUNTU finds sympathetic echoes in many non-African ideas current in contemporary writing. In particular I am thinking of ideas such as Fritz Schumacher's "small is beautiful" and "technology with a human face", Ivan Illich's "conviviality" and Simone Weil's "need for roots". Authors such as these provide terminology that could well be used to interpret the vision of UBUNTU to the contemporary world. What they have in common with UBUNTU is a perception of personal reality as the organising centre and the ultimate value of a world that is not alien to us but is our natural milieu and home. In spite of all the impersonal and dehumanising social and physical forces our century has revealed, they retain the faith that the world is for humanity and the hope that humanity can find the power to make it a home to live in as a family. Such ideas are reflected in Leopold Senghor's "cultural miscegenation" and "civilisation of the universal".

8. The struggle for a new South Africa would seem to have as its ultimate goal a more humane society in which the humanity of all is respected and developed. Surely UBUNTU has something to offer in this regard. A scientific and technological culture dominated by a theoretical and practical materialism seems to have lost touch with the humanity of its creators and controllers. We must find an alternative to materialism that is not simply dualism, an alternative to individualism that is not

some form of collectivism. Apartheid has created a culture of separation; cannot UBUNTU promote one of community? Genuine individual freedom and development and our dependence on and participation in community go together, are not opposed to each other. In every sphere of life in society this interdependence should be reflected, in a way that is special to that sphere.

In the sphere of business, for instance, UBUNTU has a great deal to offer and will have to be taken account of. It is not just that the dominant models of corporate and decision-making structures tend to prevent people with an African background from being as productive and as creative as they could be. They are subject to increasing criticism from European social scientists as well. It could well be the case that envisaging a business enterprise more on the model of an extended family—in a somewhat similar manner to that which has proved so successful in Japan—would be fruitful in developing a more holistic corporate environment, in which all employees would feel at home and able to establish an identity for themselves as members of the firm.

In the sphere of work individual creativity and the solidarity of co-operation and common ownership must go hand in hand. There should be as little as possible separation between working life and family life. Migrant labour of all kinds is contrary to the spirit of UBUNTU .

In the sphere of education equal emphasis must be placed on personal growth and service of the community. And, once again, education and family life must be integrated rather than opposed.

Health care must be based on the recognition that both health care professionals and their patients are persons first of all, and that the practice of medicine is an interpersonal transaction. Scientific and technological aspects of health care must fit in to this. In human persons there is a unity between mental and physical factors in both health and disease; one can never be treated without the other.

Although we have power to control nature we remain part of it. In all our use of it, in farming and in recreation, as well as in medicine. we have to deal with it in such a way that it becomes and remains a hospitable milieu for human life.

In the sphere of gender relations we must recognise both the equality and complementarity of men and women in every sphere of life. Work in the home should be recognised as of equal importance to work outside it and given equal financial recompense. Ideally it should not be necessary, in order to support a simple but comfortable life-style, for both parents to work outside the home when children are small. Persons are the ultimate product of society, and in this process the family has a irreplaceable role. Equality between genders should mean at least that they are equally represented numerically in the most important professions—such as education, health care, government and the police.

In all these spheres of life I feel UBUNTU has something to offer. Yet I am not uncritical of UBUNTU . In most of these spheres there is something it can learn from other different approaches. I hope our study of it will also indicate what this is.

Already the UBUNTU project is under way. The nucleus is forming. It has attracted the interest and support of various organisations and corporations. In particular I would like to mention an enlightened firm who has seen the need for such a project and has associated itself with it by means of generous sponsorship: the Old Mutual life assurance company. This company is doing all it can to bring about the integration of people from different backgrounds within a corporate culture that embodies *ubuntu* values. To this end it organises training programmes for its managers that sensitise them to different cultural frameworks, as well as facilitating critical discussion on the evolution of the culture of the firm itself. Such initiative is a strong sign of hope for the future.

Last but not least I want to acknowledge the support through many years of Andrew Tallon of the Philosophy Department at Marquette. Since we first met in 1979 we have kept in touch and it is due to him that the ideas presented in this book have been communicated to an international public, first of all in articles in his journal *Philosophy and Theology* and now here in the American edition of *Philosophy for Africa*. If the African insights are as important as I think they are, then they may have something to contribute to life in America as well.

Contents

Foreword

To one who studied Aristotelian-Thomistic philosophy nearly sixty years ago there is a lot in this book that makes it exciting. But it is not everybody's meat. A philosophical initiation is a tough apprenticeship. It certainly was in the days of my apprenticeship in the 1930's. We wrestled with the concepts of being, essence and existence, cause and effect; the good, the true, the beautiful; the Aristotelian-Thomistic theory of knowledge with its dynamic relationship of image (reflecting experience of the concrete and particular) and concept (by nature abstract and universal). Some of us even began to acquire a taste for such intellectual alpinism though the slopes we explored were often rocky and arid.

Reading what Dr. Augustine Shutte has written reveals a far more attractive vista of the Aristotelian-Thomistic scene. It takes on a human face. It becomes incarnate in the analysis of personal self-realisation and community-dependence. I have not had the leisure to study as fully as I should have liked the analysis that Shutte offers in regard to these absorbing topics, but I can always come back and read his pages again. They invite ongoing exploration.

They invite this not only for their own sake but also because of the promising encounter with African wisdom that they offer. Shutte launches an intriguing examination of the fields of contact he has discovered between this wisdom and the philosophical tradition that began with Aristotle, became a central part of western culture through Thomas Aquinas, and has been made relevant to contemporary concerns through the twentieth-century followers of these two great philosophical innovators.

In pursuing this examination Shutte recognises his debt to the great Senegalese thinker, Leopold Senghor, who pioneered this enterprise, when he noted fields of contact between African traditional values and the insights of French philosophers and visionaries like Blondel and Teilhard de Chardin.

In particular Shutte finds fields of contact between African wisdom and modern Thomism in two profound all-pervading African values: that of the life-force that permeates the universe, manifesting itself especially in human persons, and the importance of community, expressed in the Xhosa proverb, *umuntu ngumuntu ngabantu* – a person is a person because of persons.

The notion of a pervading life-force in African wisdom is not too dissimilar from that of the continuous creative influence of God in Thomistic philosophy; and as found in human beings it has a powerful kinship with the idea of the human soul or spirit which, in the philosophy of Aristotle and Aquinas, fuses with matter to constitute the human person.

Modern Thomism has built up a picture of the human person as one who achieves growing self-realisation through community relations. Free personal self-realisation is profoundly other-dependent.

Can this stir the imagination of African thinkers seeking an appropriate philosophical setting for the analysis in depth of traditional African values? Why not? This setting is an appealing one.

Appealing too for another reason: because it offers an example of how to escape from the widespread materialism of western culture. The west has enjoyed stupendous success with its scientific culture. Science operates on the basis of observation, experimentation and verification. What cannot be observed, experimented with and verified is not scientific knowledge - and therefore, to people immersed in scientific culture, all too often not strictly knowledge at all.

Africa must adopt a scientific culture if it wishes to develop but, in doing so, is it inevitable that it should sacrifice such profound truths as those contained in its own traditional ideas of vital force and community?

Dr. Shutte invites Africa to find its way out of the materialistic swamp created by our scientific culture, by marrying science to a vision of human persons achieving self-realisation in personal dependence on one another. In this way it could embrace a scientific culture while preserving the values that science, because of its very nature, cannot handle.

Inculturation is the dynamic word in Africa today, both in the religious and general cultural fields. Shutte offers an enticing model of the meeting of cultural values and philosophical reflection.

He adds further dimensions to the model by showing how it can be applied in the spheres of work and of gender relations.

He concludes his study with a brief reflection on the place of religion. He believes that, although philosophy can tell us what we should be thinking and doing, it takes religion to motivate action that fosters genuine humanity.

His book is a valuable contribution to the African intellectual and moral scene at a time when we desperately need such contributions, particularly in South Africa.

Denis E Hurley OMI
Archbishop Emeritus of Durban
July 1993

Chapter One

Philosophy and Africa

This is a book about philosophy and Africa. That philosophy and Africa should appear together in the same book might seem strange. One reason why they do so is that I am in Africa – in South Africa, to be precise – and trying to do philosophy. But there is a deeper reason: philosophy in Africa ought to be able to offer something of value to life in an African context. There would be a still deeper reason if Africa had anything that it could offer philosophy. And I think it has.

I have spoken of the African context. The context in which I write is South Africa. But South Africa is, after all, part of Africa. That is not a trivial truth. I hope its importance will appear in these pages. The present struggle in South Africa is partly a struggle between Africa and Europe. From a philosophical point of view there is a lot at issue in the meeting between African values and ways of thinking and European ones.

And not only from a philosophical point of view. The contemporary South African context is still that of the struggle against apartheid. Now however there is also talk of the "new" South Africa; the struggle is also the struggle to bring this into being. But how shall we define "new"? As democratic? Or unified? Just and peaceful? Humane? Developed? Socialist? Liberal? Capitalist? Whichever terms we choose to describe our future we had better define them carefully. The same is true if we choose to define the predicament from which we are struggling to free ourselves. What are we fighting against? Racism, poverty, non-participation, inhumanity, underdevelopment, sexism, alienation, communism? Imprecise language in this sphere can be very dangerous. There is a job for philosophy here, a job for which its tools of conceptual analysis and rational criticism are necessary.

It is not difficult to see that the question of defining the character of the new South Africa is one in which our deepest values are at stake. We are concerned to know what is good and what is possible, with human needs and human abilities. Our whole conception of persons, what they are and what they need in order to develop and find fulfilment, is involved. Here too there is a need for rigorous reflection on what the past has taught us, and careful criticism of the alternatives that are offered us for the future. And this, if anything, is what philosophy has always tried to do.

The "moment of truth" for philosophy

I teach philosophy as an academic subject in a South African university, and so I have to face the question of the value and importance of philosophy in a South African context. Philosophy, as I hope to show, is the search for truths and values that are true and valuable for every place and time. But like every human activity it must take place in a particular place and time, growing out of a particular tradition of thought and writing that is different from other traditions, and dealing with issues and problems that are experienced in a particular social and cultural situation that is different from every other. The philosophical tradition that I and most other South African philosophers stand in is the European one – in which I include also the English and the American. But our experience is African. The universal human predicament that philosophy tries to understand is made concrete for us in our own society, in South Africa at the end of the twentieth century.

If my doing philosophy is to be authentic – not "just" an academic exercise but part of my real life – then it must be in touch with, and an attempt to understand, the only life that can be real for me, which is the one that is rooted in South Africa in the 1990s as I write. Academics are also human beings, and it is more important to be good at being human than good at philosophy. Being an academic is justified only if it serves humanity in some way or other, and society is justified in requiring this of us. If philosophy is a worthwhile activity it must prove its worth in the human context that supports it and makes it possible. In this book I will try to do this in the context of South Africa.

Academic philosophy in South Africa has not yet proved its human worth. By and large we academic philosophers have taken refuge from the struggle in the streets and townships and shut ourselves up in our "ivory towers". But there is another problem with philosophy in a South African context. It has nothing to do with academics as such, but with the kind of philosophy we do, the particular tradition in which most of us stand. It is of course a

European tradition, but more precisely it is the Anglo-American analytical part of that tradition, a style of philosophy that became popular in Oxford and Cambridge in the early part of this century and was then exported to America and other English-speaking countries, so that it is now the most influential philosophical school or movement in the world. This is the kind of philosophy that seems unwilling or unable to engage with the human issues that arise in our present context in South Africa. Why should that be so?

As this book is my attempt to overcome this inability and unwillingness, I hope that it will provide a fairly detailed answer to this question. But I will make the main points here. Anglo-American philosophy has developed hand-in-glove with science, especially the natural sciences, and has been deeply influenced in its aims and values and methods by science and the environment and culture that science and technology have produced. As a consequence it has come to see itself either as an aspect of science, or else just as philosophy of science, a second-order activity having science rather than the real world as its object of study. In either case, it is understood to be science and not philosophy that gives us knowledge of reality; philosophy merely helps us organise our scientific ideas and methods better. The result is that this kind of philosophy loses touch with experience and the world itself. Even more importantly, it loses touch with action and the world of values. Science is "value-free", and so philosophy must be too.

In this way the two most important parts of traditional philosophy, metaphysics (our overall view of the world or reality) and ethics (our fundamental system of values), are abandoned. Contemporary Anglo-American analytical philosophy does in fact inculcate a general view of the world and values; it is materialist, liberal-capitalist, utilitarian and atheist. I hope to indicate some of the errors in such an outlook in what follows. But, mistaken or not, the most important defect in this style of philosophy is its failure to provide an understanding of our own humanity of the kind traditionally aimed at by philosophy, the kind of understanding that enables us to give some objective answer to our most pressing questions concerning meaning and value.

Whatever the correctness of such criticisms, the fact remains that this kind of philosophy does not engage in a systematic way with the the most fundamental questions and issues of life, as these appear to the vast majority of humanity. Whether this failure owes something to the socio-economic setting in which it developed (liberal, capitalist, industrialised) is not of prime importance. Every philosophy must grow up in a particular setting. But a successful philosophy is one that is able to grasp what is universally true in the particular circumstances of its setting. And my view, for which I shall argue in the following pages, is that this style of philosophy has overlooked something of crucial importance to humanity in whatever context it finds itself. It is for this reason that it has been so far of little help in the struggle in South Africa.

What has brought me to this view has been my own recent experience of Africa, or, if that sounds odd coming from one who was born and brought up in Africa, it has been my own recent awakening to African thought, African values and African culture through my encounters with black colleagues and students, black fellow-parishioners of a township church, and philosophy written by black authors in Africa. In all these forms I found the African tradition to be alive and full of things to teach me.

What has especially struck me as a philosopher is the conception of human nature and human flourishing that is embodied in traditional African thought and practices and institutions. I have become convinced that this insight into our humanity can serve as an important corrective to contemporary European philosophy, both in the form that I have just criticised, and in its other presently dominant form, the Marxist socialist one.

In particular the traditional African conception of community (as expressed in such proverbs as *umuntu ngumuntu ngabantu* – a person depends on persons to be a person) and that of the fundamental energy of the universe (*seriti*) as being neither purely material nor purely spiritual, hold out hope that the eternal conflict in European philosophy between individalism and collectivism on the one hand, and materialism and dualism on the other, might not be eternal after all.

Of course such traditional conceptions have not, by and large, undergone rigorous philosophical scrutiny and assessment. Traditional thought simply assumed their coherence and truth and did not seek to systematise or prove them. Philosophy as a rigorous, self-critical intellectual discipline is a comparative newcomer to modern Africa. But in the last thirty or forty years significant attempts have been made by African philosophers to subject such traditional conceptions to philosophical analysis and systematisation.

One such attempt, that of Leopold Senghor in Senegal, I have found particularly instructive and take as something of a model. He uses the European philosophy in which he has been trained (French in his case) to give contemporary expression to those insights inherited from his African past which he considers to have a universal value.

Such creative interpenetration of European and African thought as one finds in writers like Senghor is just what I feel is needed in a South African context, both for the sake of philosophy and for the sake of South Africa. If philosophy has anything to offer the new South Africa it must be a philosophy that is engaged in South African reality. Part of that reality is traditional African thought about the meaning and value of human life. I think this should be reflected in our philosophy too.

The aim of this book

The kernel of this book, then, is my attempt to outline a philosophical conception of humanity that incorporates and systematises the African insights I think so important. I use the particular European philosophical tradition in which I have been trained for this purpose. It is the tradition in which Aristotle and Aquinas are the classical figures, but in recent times it has incorporated into itself elements of existentialism and phenomenology and even of linguistic philosophy of the kind asociated with the later Wittgenstein. In many ways this tradition has been at odds with the dominant schools of contemporary philosophy, especially in the English-speaking world, though at the time of writing it seems to be experiencing something of an increase in popularity in academic circles. More important though, for my purpose, are certain points of similarity, both as regards content and as regards overall structure, between it and traditional African thought, particularly as concerns our understanding of human nature and morality.

Two crucial points of similarity between contemporary Thomist philosophy and traditional African thought can be found in the conviction that human persons transcend the realm of the merely material, and also that in order to develop as persons we need to be empowered by others.

At first sight these two insights appear to contradict each other. The first is the foundation of our freedom, as originators of thought and action, from total determination by external causes of the kind that the sciences can discover; the second affirms our complete dependence on other persons for our own development. In spite of the apparent contradiction I try to show that the paradox of freedom-in-dependence does indeed express an important truth about human nature.

I do this by showing how it is precisely our capacity for free self-realisation that requires *a certain kind* of influence of other persons if it is to develop towards fulfilment. This development is presented in three stages: from the basic capacity for self-consciousness and self-determination that makes us persons, through increasing self-knowledge and self-affirmation, to a progressively greater ability for self-transcendence and self-donation in our relationships with others. The whole process is made possible by virtue by a complex interpersonal transaction with other persons. Individual freedom and community with others need not be seen as opposed, but only on condition that one understands the way in which persons transcend the realm of the merely material.

Working out a philosophy of persons and personal development that incorporates a traditional African conception of humanity, is also a way of dealing with the opposition in European philosophy between both materialism and dualism and individualism and collectivism. The interpersonal transaction that brings about personal growth in us reveals a kind of personal energy or power that is certainly not physical in any way, but which is embodied and expressed in physical reality. And the fact that individual freedom is shown to depend on personal relationships with others for its exercise, growth and fulfilment provides us with an alternative to both an individualistic and a collectivist approach to society and politics.

The main practical task of the book is to show that philosophy can provide insight and guidance in the present predicament in which we find ourselves in South Africa. The first half of the book is taken up with constructing the philosophy, the second with applying it.

There is first of all the task of describing the predicament we are in. The South African situation has elements that are unique, but it also has many that are common to it and the rest of Africa. Africa as a whole has much in common with the rest of the Third World. Finally there are features that define a predicament in which the whole world stands at the end of the twentieth century. Can philosophy throw light on this?

I argue that it can. Our philosophical account of persons and the necessary conditions of personal growth can direct our attention to those aspects of the contemporary world that prevent these conditions from being realised. It can also sensitise us to the fundamental source of the problem in the depths of human nature: our capacity and desire for freedom, and our dependence on others for its development and fulfilment. This is the root of the human drama and the key to understanding the particular forms it takes in our own time and country.

Within this philosophical framework we look at the world-wide opposition between the "developed" and the "undeveloped" countries, and the conflicts created by apartheid in South Africa. We are helped in this by accounts of the 'African predicament' already produced by African philosophers to whose work I refer. I then try to show how these conflicts can be seen as the results of mistaken and self-defeating attempts at self-realisation through self-assertion. Alternatively they can be seen as attempts at achieving liberation on the part of countries, groups and individuals, that are vitiated by a false conception of the conditions for human freedom that encourages a misguided desire for total independence.

I then address the question of how the predicament may be overcome, and argue that philosophy has a distinctive contribution to make in this connection. It is in the sphere of ethics, namely that concerning the goals and aims of the struggle for freedom, the human qualities and standards that should characterise its conduct, and the kind of methods that may be employed, where philosophy must make its contribution.

First of all philosophy can help in defining the necessary conditions for human development and fulfilment. The key idea that persons can only develop as persons in relationships with others in which self-knowledge and self-affirmation are fostered and increased, provides a fundamental standard for the practices, the institutions and the culture that constitute our society. This standard can be made more concrete by spelling out the qualities of character and the kinds of relationship that both express and foster the development of persons.

This basic understanding of persons and personal community can then be applied to the different spheres of life in society, in order to see in some detail what is required in each sphere of life if personal growth and community is to be promoted rather than hindered. As an example of such applied philosophy I look in particular at the spheres of work and gender relations.

Finally we address the most important question of all, the practical question. Even if philosophy has given us a clear understanding of our predicament and helped us to see what we ought to do in order to overcome it, we still have to do it. And in order to do it we have to want to do it. If philosophy shows us anything it shows us this: that we don't want to do it, or we don't want to enough! The final problem is the problem of our wanting. That has to undergo a change of character.

Philosophy can't do that for us. I argue that this is the role of religion. It is only religion that can *empower* us to overcome a predicament of this kind. Nevertheless even here philosophy has a role, though a subordinate one, to play. In South Africa it is quite clear that religion is part of the problem. The separation and opposition that characterise our country show themselves in the sphere of religion too. There is separation and opposition between different religions, between different denominations of the same religion, and within each denomination too. Religious life is just as much a "site of struggle" as anywhere else.

In spite of that I argue that the only solution to our predicament is a religious one. A genuine dialogue between the different religions and denominations must begin. But it must be a *religious* dialogue, not one of another kind. A religious dialogue involves a person as a whole; no part of their life or being is left out. Only an encounter of this kind can provide the human medium for the kind of power that is necessary to change our hearts. Without new hearts, no new South Africa.

Such religious dialogue is absolutely necessary if the struggle in South Africa is to be effective. It cannot take the place of the efforts that must be made in the other spheres of life, but without it their success will not be enduring. I said that philosophy has a role, though a subordinate one, even in the sphere of religion. It is this: dialogue requires a common language. Each religious tradition has its own. A condition for real commitment to dialogue is the readiness to sacrifice familiar and much-loved expressions for the sake of mutual understanding. This is where philosophy can help: in the translation of the doctrines of particular religious traditions into a language that expresses a common understanding of the humanity that all believers have in common. This must be possible. And if possible, it should be done.

The structure of this book

The above account of what I am aiming at in will explain the sequence of chapters and the structure of this book.

In the next chapter, I introduce the topic of philosophy, its nature, aims and method, with a brief discussion of the history of philosophy in Africa and the present thinking of contemporary African philosophers on the subject. The whole question of the relation between philosophy and traditional African thought is highly controversial, and I want to make my own position absolutely clear.

The third chapter of the book is a synoptic account of another attempt to do more or less what I attempt, that of Senghor. I describe in some detail his attempt to develop his philosophy of "negritude" out of traditional African thought using the philosophy of Teilhard de Chardin.

I then turn to a critical assessment of the dominant forms of contemporary European philosophy, the gist of which I have indicated above. This leads to a fairly extended treatment of traditional African thought that is focussed on the two key conceptions I have already mentioned, *umuntu ngumuntu ngabantu* and *seriti*.

The next three chapters contain my own attempt at a philosophical account of persons and personal development that gives the African insights a systematic and critical foundation.

The first of these is a discussion of the European philosophical tradition in which I write, namely that of Aristotle and Aquinas, as well as contemporary Thomist philosophers such as Rahner and Lonergan and others. In the second I set out my own formulation of a conception of humanity in a summary but systematic way. In the third I highlight the way in which this conception provides an alternative to both materialism and dualism, while at the same time avoiding the individualism and collectivism criticised in previous chapters.

The final chapters of the book consist of an attempt to apply this conception of humanity to the contemporary predicament in Africa, and especially in South Africa, as I understand it.

The first of these, Chapter Nine, deals with the notion of a human predicament as such. Are there common features in the predicaments in which human individuals or groups get involved, whatever special sorts they be: sexual, marital, ecomomic, political or religious? Can a philosophical understanding of human nature reveal general problematic features of human existence that would constitute the human predicament as such? If so, can it indicate the necessary conditions that would have to be met if such a predicament is to be overcome? I give an affirmative answer to these three questions. Human persons have the capacity for free self-realisation in personal community with others. In various ways, in various spheres of life, in various societies and cultures, this freedom and community is denied, suppressed, destroyed. We use our philosophy of persons to outline a theory of liberation that offers criteria for human freedom in different concrete spheres of life.

In Chapter Ten we consider the problem of liberation in a contemporary African, and especially South African, context.

In Chapters Eleven and Twelve we apply our general theory of liberation to, respectively, the spheres of work and gender relations, in order to illustrate the criteria it would generate in those particular spheres, and how they might be embodied in a liberation struggle.

Finally, in Chapter Thirteen, we consider religion as that crucial sphere of life in which the actual commitment to liberation must be made.

Chapter Two

Philosophy in Africa

There is at present (and has been for at least the past twenty years) a conversation continuing between representatives of different disciplines on the topic of African philosophy. It comprises many different questions but all have something to do with the nature of philosophy and its position and importance in the African world.

H. O. Oruka (an African philosopher teaching in Africa in the twentieth century) in a paper, 'Four Trends in Current African Philosophy', (1978) presented at a conference on William Amo (an African philosopher who taught in Germany in the eighteenth century), distinguishes four different meanings that can be given to the expression "African philosophy".

1. Ethno-philosophy. This term, coined by Kwame Nkrumah, describes a world-view or system of thought of a particular African community or language group or even of the whole of Africa. Strictly speaking ethno-philosophy only acquires systematic written formulation in the works of modern writers (Senghor and Tempels for instance) who combine the knowledge of African traditional thought and a European philosophical education in their work.

2. Individual wisdom. This is the wisdom of wise persons in traditional culture who, though illiterate, are "critical independent thinkers who guide their thought and judgments by the power of reason and inborn insight rather than by the authority of the communal consensus." (1978)

3. Nationalist-ideological philosophy. This refers to the attempts by contemporary political theorists, such as Nyerere and Kaunda, to produce a "new and, if possible, unique political theory based on traditional African socialism and familyhood" (Bodunrin, 1981). Such theories are not narrowly political but attempt to deal with all aspects of human life in the spirit of traditional African "humanism".

4. Professional philosophy. This is the work of academics educated in Western philosophy but who belong to African universities and are in intellectual contact with each other. Such an African philosophical tradition is only just beginning.

Two different approaches

As I have said contemporary discussion of African philosophy is focussed on both the nature of philosophy, and its position and importance in Africa. If philosophy is defined by its method – rigorous, analytical, critical let us say – then professional philosophy in universities becomes the centre of interest. If it is defined by its content – theories of the nature of the universe, of the mind, of death, as well as theories of society and morality – then traditional African thought has a great deal to offer that is of philosophical interest.

Representative of the former approach are such writers as Bodunrin, Wiredu, Oruka and Hountondji. They are all academics trained in European or American universities, are in close intellectual touch with each other, and write on topics common in contemporary Anglo-American analytical philosophy. They do not deny that philosophy is, and should be, influenced by the cultural context in which it is produced. Both the type of concern that excites enquiry and hence the content of the theses that emerge from this are influenced by the social and political context. It is important for African philosophers to be sensitive to the specific situation in which they write. Apart from anything else there is the inevitable influence of language on thought. The availability of concepts depends on the common language and a philosopher must be critically aware of this.

Wiredu writes of a need "to fashion philosophies based upon common African experience with its many-sidedness", and holds that "the term "African philosophy" should be reserved for the results of that enterprise" (1980: 36). Nevertheless he intends this in a sense that would apply equally to philosophy in America or England. There is no special need in Africa for philosophy to be "archaeological" or "anthropological". African philosophy is almost wholly the product of people who are writing today; in fact African philosophy is still in the process of construction.

As I have said, the writers in this group conceive of philosophy primarily in terms of its method. What distinguishes their work in an African context is the application of a novel method in dealing with issues that are both traditional and universal. A second group of writers is more concerned with the actual doctrines contained in traditional African thought and aims to examine them in a strictly philosophical way. This group includes writers such as Gyekye, Kagame, Tempels and Ruch. Their work relies heavily on the work of anthropologists and linguists as well as on oral tradition – stories and myths and proverbs. Their aim however is philosophical. For Gyekye "Philosophy is a conceptual response to basic human problems at different epochs" (1987: 39). And so he defines African philosophy as follows: "A philosophical discourse that critically interacts or communes with African cultural and intellectual experiences, with African mentalities and traditions, will be African" (1987: 211). The context in which the philosopher works is temporal as well as spatial; it includes the history that has formed him as well as the contemporary social and political environment. For this reason "the starting points, the organizing concepts and categories of modern African philosophy (should) be extracted from the cultural, linguistic and historical background of African peoples, if that philosophy is to have relevance and meaning for the people, if it is to enrich their lives" (1987: 42). Gyekye is not only concerned that contemporary African philosophy should be in continuity and grow out of traditional African thought. That is a necessity if philosophy is to be an intellectual response to a *particular* context. He is equally concerned that the philosophy should be "extracted" from this tradition. Traditional conceptions must be given "adequate philosophical formulation, articulation and analysis by modern African philosophers" (1987: 41).

Two different conceptions of philosophy

Underlying these two different approaches to the question of African philosophy are two different understandings of philosophy itself. The first emphasizes the universality of philosophical truth and even of philosophical method; the second stresses the fact that actual philosophy is always produced in a particular culture and language and develops particular sets of concepts to deal with particular intellectual problems that are felt to be important.

The first understanding of philosophy sees philosophy as inextricably bound up with science, as being in fact scientific. This is the view of most contemporary Anglo-American philosophers and is certainly the view of the African philosophers I am speaking of. Wiredu is typical of this attitude when he writes "I take science to be the crucial factor in the transition from the traditional to the modern world. All developing nations are endeavouring to improve their living standards through the application of science, and any philosophy not thoroughly imbued with the spirit of science cannot hope to reflect this" (1980: 32). For him scientific method is the paradigm of all good intellectual activity. "If a scientific outlook is an urgent necessity at the practical level of national life, it is hardly reasonable to exempt the philosopher from the need to evince similar qualities in his abstract meditations" (1980: 32). This leads him to urge that modern African philosophers "acquire a training in methods of scientifically orientated philosophical thinking of the type evolved where scientific and technological advance has been greatest" (1980: 33).

There is a danger in this attitude: its too enthusiastic admiration of the methods and achievements of science. It is insufficiently critical of the limitations of scientific knowledge. Sometimes it even identifies scientific knowledge as the only knowledge worth having – or even the only knowledge that there is. This is a serious mistake and one that can have disastrous consequences, as I shall presently try to show. One can see the temptation for philosophers in developing countries to idolise science and technology, but such an attitude is the enemy of both philosophy and of genuine development.

On the other hand this attitude has a good grasp on the universality of philosophical truth. If it is true that the human mind is material or that the human will is free then it is true of all human beings wherever they happen to live. There may well be all sorts of culturally conditioned insights into and ways of understanding materiality or freedom, but if there is a fact of the matter (as there certainly is for this understanding of philosophy), then some just are better or more adequate then others.

It is certainly the case that a scientific-technological culture is re-colonising the world. Apart from the promise of development this contains there is the opportunity it creates for world-wide communication. Real relativism regarding the fundamental metaphysical and ethical insights available to humanity can only be the enemy of such communication. The universality of philosophical truth is the essential antidote to such relativism.

There is a danger in the second attitude as well; it is precisely the danger of relativism. The idea that truth is always and only "true for me" is not only mistaken but, when it comes to important metaphysical and ethical issues, clears a space for all sorts of ideological and political demons. Ideas about what is "genuinely African" can be used to justify all sorts of injustice and as a smokescreen to hide the struggle for political power. And, as Wiredu points out, one of the essential practical effects of genuine philosophy is to overcome the irrationality embodied in the varieties of anachronism, authoritarianism and superstition that prevent the proper development of African countries.

On the other hand the second attitude recognises the particular cultural roots of *any* philosophical system, including those produced in the scientific culture of Europe. This is something that Anglo-American (and European) philosophers tend to forget. Or else they really do believe that "scientific" philosophy is an exception to this rule. And this is a mistake caused by their attachment to science. Science, at least the natural sciences, can be free of cultural particularity in a way that philosophy can't be. This is because of its mathematical nature. Of course the maths involved in, say, physics, is the product of European culture, but its meaning, the meaning of the symbols used, is something both stipulated and precise. It can take no other form and must be simply learnt. Philosophy, for reasons I shall presently suggest, cannot be like that. So it can't have the kind of universality that science has, a rigorous universality of expression. The physical embodiment of this kind of universality is of course the instrument, the recording or measuring device which is constructed precisely in order to be sensitive to a specific element of physical reality.

If it is true (and surely the human sciences have shown us that it is) that all thought is situated in and influenced by its cultural context, then philosophers better be aware of that fact. Indeed, if philosophy's field includes the assumptions that underlie all our contemplative and active life, then an investigation of the fundamental categories and concepts from which these assumptions are made up is a necessary task. And these are always present in some or other particular form, determined by the history and circumstances of a people, which has already formed the mind of the would-be philosopher. It is impossible to reflect on one's experience to any depth unless one begins with a critical analysis of the concepts and categories in terms of which it has already been understood. For English persons to root their own philosophy in a study of Akan or Yoruba thought (or Greek or Latin thought for that matter) without ever referring it to the concepts and categories they have inherited and made their own simply by virtue of living in a particular cultural context, would be to prevent themselves for ever from connecting their thought with reality as they experience it. Their philosophy, as a result, is bound to remain merely academic and so superficial. Whatever doctrines it may contain, they have done the one thing necessary to avoid the possibility of establishing their truth. Though some of them may happen to be true, they have not tested their truth against the reality of their own experience. And the same goes for the African who "learns" philosophy from an American text-book. Unless the world of the text-book engages in their mind with the world of their childhood, their thought will inhabit two different worlds and neither will be real. Philosophy resulting from such mental schizophrenia will not contain much truth. On the other hand the attempt to use European philosophical tools and techniques on traditional African conceptual systems might – in addition to producing an African philosopher – result in a philosophical "discovery" or creation that would otherwise have never happened.

In spite of the difference of approach between these two groups of African philosophers, one seeing philosophy more in terms of its special method, the other more in terms of the themes and topics it deals with, they are united in the belief that philosophy has an important intellectual function in the context of contemporary Africa. In order to decide whether they are right about this one has first to come to a decision about the true nature and function of philosophy and about the nature of the problems of contemporary Africa that philosophy so conceived could appropriately tackle. In the rest of this book I will try to make up my mind about both these matters.

I think philosophy needs to be defined both by its method and by its content. I will presently explain why. It is because of this that my interest in philosophy in Africa can be expressed by two distinct questions. Can traditional African thought be of help to contemporary philosophy? I think it can. And can contemporary philosophy be of help to Africa? I think it can. I also think the two questions are connected. It is only when it allows itself to learn from traditional African thought that contemporary philosophy will be able to give Africa the help she really needs and which is its proper task to give.

I now propose to describe in some detail the attempt of the Senegalese philosopher and statesman, Leopold Senghor, to bring together in a creative synthesis European philosophy and traditional African ideas. His motive in this attempt was twofold. On the one hand he was convinced that traditional

African thought embodied insights into human nature and the nature of knowledge that the dominant forms of European philosophy had forgotten or ignored. And on the other he realised that if the inevitable mixing of European and African culture (attendant on the spread of European science and technology) was to preserve the genuine human values of both traditions, an integration at the conceptual level (especially as regards an understanding of human nature and human values) was a necessity.

Chapter Three

A Pioneer: Leopold Senghor

Senghor's thought develops against the background of French colonialism in Africa. That situation determines the ultimate aims of his intellectual life. He wishes most of all to overcome that loss of identity suffered by Africans due to a history of slavery, colonialism and racism. And so he argues first of all for political independence. But this is only a first step towards a more comprehensive freedom of spirit which he wants for himself and his fellow Africans. The second step is to initiate a cultural rebellion against the French policy of cultural assimilation of their colonies to metropolitan France. To this end his main intellectual work is to define and foster the idea of "negritude". Negritude he defines as "the whole complex of civilised values – cultural, economic, social and political – which characterise the black peoples, or, more precisely, the Negro-African world" (1963: 11). What these are we shall presently see. Here it is important to note Senghor's reasons for going to work in this way.

His main reason is his conviction that traditional African culture has something of great, and unique, value to offer to a future "civilisation of the universal" which he recognises to be a necessity if there is to be peace between nations and the gap between developed and undeveloped nations is to be overcome. Senghor is, as we shall see, extremely critical of contemporary European culture, though deeply indebted to it, and feels that it needs the help that Africa can give. This negritude is able to supply as a kind of complement to European ideas and values; it will make up something that is presently lacking. On the other hand Senghor is quite clear that Africa needs what Europe has to offer, and not only in the realm of science and technology and the organisation of society. New developments in European scientific thinking and philosophy provide precisely the intellectual tools suitable for developing the idea of negritude in a systematic and detailed way. Negritude is not simply an archaeology of ancient values but a new creation out of traditional materials; thus it needs modern tools.

I now propose to explain briefly Senghor's main criticisms of European culture and thought, before setting out in some detail how he uses particular developments in European philosophy and science, especially the work of Teilhard de Chardin, to articulate his conception of negritude to the full. In the course of this I hope to give a clear idea of the characteristics of negritude as well as a more specific idea of how Senghor thinks this will help towards the creation of a "civilisation of the universal".

Senghor's critique of Europe

Senghor's chief criticism of European culture is directed at its materialism. This is present in both capitalism and communism and makes a true understanding of persons and a truly human society impossible. Theoretical and practical materialism is born from the application of scientific reason to every aspect of life. Science is incapable of understanding even matter properly; it is quite inadequate for dealing with humanity. Marxism, though praised for its (limited) use of a new "dialectical" method, comes in for special criticism for its determinism and atheism, as also for its idea of class struggle. For Senghor the chief economic problem is "not to eliminate classes by a class struggle within the nation; it is to bridge the gap between developed and undeveloped nations" (1965: 143).

The full force of Senghor's criticism of European culture appears, oddly enough, in connection with his account of that part of European culture, of European thought in particular, which he feels is indispensable for the development of negritude, the way of thinking he calls "dialectical". We must now consider this in some detail.

Dialectics, in Senghor's terminology, is contrasted with the naive realism and positivism in philosophy that grew up in connection with the natural sciences, and reigned supreme as a theory of knowledge until mid-way through the nineteenth century. It produces a general attitude to reality that is the opposite of the mechanistic and deterministic materialism that it supplants. "This new method ... is born of the new scientific revolutions: relativity, wave mechanics, quantum theory, para-Euclidean geometry, theories of the discontinuous and undetermined. And also from the new philosophical revolutions: phenomenology, existentialism, Teilhardism" (1965: 70).

In spite of this indication of the origins of dialectical method, which admittedly does communicate the character of the method in its contemporary setting, Senghor usually locates its origin in the dialectics of Hegel. He then praises Marx and Engels for taking over the method, but criticises them for failing to grasp its full import and so remaining materialists. Indeed it is precisely the scientific discoveries listed above that reveal the inadequacies of materialism: "the discoveries since Engels' death – of relativity, quantum mechanics, wave mechanics, relations of uncertainty – have upset the materialist and determinist metaphysics of Marx and Engels" (1965: 133). He quotes Bachelard with approval when he asserts that "The qualities of the scientific real are thus, primarily, the functions of our rational methods", understanding this to imply that scientists "suspect that the most minute particles of matter – photons, protons and electrons – have no reality outside of our thinking." He concludes that "dialectics and consequently knowledge is essentially an *elan* of the mind ... How far we now are from the 'reflection', from the 'copy'! This is a dialectical turn that almost rehabilitates Hegel" (1965: 150).

In general, dialectics, for Senghor, is any method of knowledge that involves the creative engagment of the subject with the object of his study. He speaks of a "knowledge by confrontation and intuition" (1965: 72). "It is essentially in the confrontation of the subject and the object – and vice versa – that one finds dialectical logic, the act of knowledge, which is at once theory and practice. By *theory* I mean the 'categories' of understanding, and, by *practice*, the methods and techniques of the subject" (1965: 150). He stresses the active, creative character of knowing; it is a practical activity, not merely a contemplative gaze: "to know an object, it no longer suffices to see it, to dissect it, to weigh it, even if one has the most perfect precision instruments. One must also touch it, penetrate it from the inside – so to speak – and finger it" (1965: 71).

This understanding of knowledge is especially relevant to the knowledge of humanity and the human sciences: "To know a human fact, psychological or social, no longer means to investigate it with the aid of statistics and graphs, but to live it: like the white man who, to understand the situation of Negro Americans, blackened his skin with a chemical product and worked as a Negro shoe-shine boy. This is what phenomenological or existential thought reveals, as it follows the path of Marxism and exceeds it while integrating it. In this school of thought, the real coincides with thought, the content of a statement coincides with the form in which it is expressed, philosophy blends with science, as art merges with existence, with life" (1965: 71).

Understanding knowledge in this way clearly has implications of a metaphysical kind. The fact that one can't separate the knower from the known entails that one cannot make a distinction between two kinds of reality, one purely mental, the other merely material. Similarly, the undermining of mechanism and determinism makes the world appear as "a discontinuous and perhaps undetermined reality" (1965: 70), the work and the home of freedom. The world as a whole, including humanity, is dynamic, developing, and human freedom is part of this dynamism of development.

For Senghor it is the discovery of this dialectical method for acquiring knowledge of ourselves and the world that has shown up the true inadequacies of European scientific-technological culture. On the other hand it is precisely this new way of thinking that makes a bridge between European culture and negritude and provides the necessary intellectual tool for expressing the insights of traditional African thought in a systematic way. "On closer scrutiny", he writes, "this knowledge by confrontation and intuition is Negro-African knowledge ... From our ancestors we have inherited our own method of knowledge. Why should we change it when Europeans now tell us it is the very method of the twentieth century – and the most fruitful method?" He then proceeds to describe the traditional African method of knowing in some detail:

"In contrast to the classic European, the Negro African does not draw a line between himself and the object; he does not hold it at a distance, nor does he merely look at it and analyse it ... He touches it, feels it, smells it ... Subjectively, at the tips of his sensory organs, his insect antennas, he discovers the Other. Immediately he is moved, going centrifugally from subject to object on the waves of the Other ... Thus the Negro African 'sympathizes', feels with, abandons his personality to become identified with the Other, dies to be reborn in the Other. He does not assimilate; he is assimilated. He lives a common life with the Other; he lives in a symbiosis ... Subject and object are dialectically face to face in the very act of knowledge."

To the objection that he is reducing knowledge to emotion and denying the role of reason, he replies as follows: "However paradoxical it may seem, the vital force of the Negro African, his surrender to the object, is animated by reason. Let us understand each other clearly; it is not the reasoning-eye of Europe, it is the reason of the touch, better still, the reasoning-embrace, the sympathetic reason, more closely related to the Greek *logos* than to the Latin *ratio* ... European reasoning is analytical, discursive by utilization; Negro African reasoning is intuitive by participation" (1965: 73 –74).

Such descriptions echo, in a more poetic way, everything he has had to say about European dialectic. In his desire to provide a contemporary systematic philosophical account of the insights and values of negritude, he therefore seizes on dialectic as the most suitable intellectual tool. Method of knowledge and conception of reality hang together; dialectic ought therefore to be capable of giving a contemporary account of the traditional African vision of the world and the values of human life. Of all European thinkers who use this method Teilhard de Chardin, Senghor feels, comes closest to establishing a philosophical system that incorporates the African insights.

Traditional African thought

Before I give an account of how Senghor uses de Chardin I will briefly enumerate what Senghor takes to be the important characteristics of traditional African thought that must be retained in any contemporary system of negritude.

Like all African philosophers he recognises certain ideas as fundamental to traditional African wisdom: that reality is force and the world a process of interplay between forces, that humanity is part of this universal field of force, that at bottom all force is alive, spiritual rather than material, that the individual's life and fulfilment are only to be found in community with others (a community that does not end at death), that morality is the development of natural tendencies to fuller being and more abundant life, and finally that all human life and world process is directed and empowered by a transcendent origin of life and force. The following two quotations give us an idea of Senghor's own attachment to this vision:

"Far back as one may go into his past, from the Northern Soudanese to the Southern Bantu, the African has always and everywhere presented a concept of the world which is diametrically opposed to the traditional philosophy of Europe. The latter is essentially static, objective, dichotomous; it is, in fact, dualistic, in that it makes an absolute distinction between body and soul, matter and spirit. It is founded on separation and opposition, on analysis and conflict. The African, on the other hand, conceives the world, beyond the diversity of its forms, as a fundamentally mobile yet unique reality that seeks synthesis ... This reality is being in the ontological sense of the word, and it is life force. For the African, matter in the sense the Europeans understand it, is only a system of signs which translates the single reality of the universe: being, which is spirit, which is life force. Thus, the whole universe appears as an infinitely small, and at the same time infinitely large, network of life forces which emanate from God and end in God, who is the source of all life forces. It is He who vitalizes and devitalizes all other beings, all the other life forces" (1966: 4).

"Negritude ... as a complex of civilized values, is traditionally socialist in character ... It is a community based society ... communal, not collectivist. We are concerned here, not with a mere collection of individuals, but with people conspiring together, *con – spiring* in the basic Latin sense, united among themselves even to the very centre of their being, communing through their ancestors with God, who is the Centre of all centres" (1963: 16).

There is nothing new in this inventory of the characteristics of negritude. What is new in Senghor's contemporary synthesis however, is his application of the traditional wisdom far beyond the traditional situation to take in the whole international scene, and the future as well as the present.

Combining the African ideas, especially those of community, of morality as the drive to fuller being, and God as the source and goal of all life force, Senghor develops a theory of the tendency of all peoples to communicate, to merge and eventually to become a universal community. This is what he understands by African socialism; he calls it "the civilization of the universal". "The means of socialism transcend mere physical comfort, even on the national level; they are already personal values, values of the fuller being ... Today, ships and railways, aeroplanes and rockets, books and newspapers, radio and television, are all more than means to an international economy, they are *values* of the Civilization of the Universal" (1963: 21).

Because of this Africa has a special part to play in the construction of this international community, a moral part. "Beyond the objective of material well-being, Man aspires to fuller being, which is his end; beyond the satisfaction of his material needs, to that of his spiritual needs. Especially in black Africa and in the underdeveloped countries. Their peoples hunger not so much after American or Russian surpluses, as after independence, dignity, science and culture: after *Love-in-Union*. Try to imagine a world without love: between man and wife, in the family, in the nation, on the whole planet. Without this Love-in-Union, which is made real in God, through religion and art, the world would be ice-bound; we would be powerless to prevent the *taedium vitae* taking possession of our souls" (1963: 21). The insights of traditional African thought into the human need for community and the values it entails are precisely what are needed to direct the world-wide process of socialization.

This is the culmination of Senghor's theory of negritude and his conception of the role that Africa can play in the future. "I would like to emphasize at this point how much these characteristics of negritude enable it to find its place in contemporary humanism, thereby permitting black Africa to make its contribution to the 'Civilization of the Universal' which is so necessary in our divided but interdependent world of the second half of the 20th century. A contribution, first of all, to international co-operation, which must be and shall be the cornerstone of that civilization. It is through these virtues of negritude that decolonization has been accomplished without too much bloodshed or hatred and that a positive form of co-operation based on 'dialogue and reciprocity' has been established between former colonizers and colonized. It is through these virtues that there has been a new spirit at the United Nations, where the 'no' and the bang of the fist on the table are no longer signs of strength. It is through these virtues that peace through co-operation could extend to South Africa, Rhodesia and the Portuguese colonies, if only the dualistic spirit of the Whites would open itself to dialogue" (1966: 5).

The Civilisation of the Universal will not result from the extension of European culture across the globe, though that is certainly inevitable, but from what Senghor calls, in a striking phrase, "biological and psychic miscegenation, a process of entering into personal communion that African thought so well understands and values." "The Civilization of the Universal, which will be the culmination of socialization, will not be European civilization – in either its Eastern or Western form – imposed by force, but a biological and psychic miscegenation, a *sym-biosis* of the different civilizations" (1963: 22).

A synthesis: Senghor and Teilhard

We are now in a position to see how the work of Teilhard de Chardin enabled Senghor to gather the insights of traditional African thought into a coherent system and what is more, bring those insights to bear on the post-colonial predicament of Africa – and the world itself as well.

We have already become acquainted with Senghor's notion of dialectic as a method of knowledge more consonant with the scientific advances of the twentieth century. In his eyes Teilhard de Chardin, both as a scientist and as philosopher, clearly exemplifies this method. "It was on the basis of these discoveries, through a combination of logical coherence and amazing intuition, of scientific experiment and inner experience, that Pierre Teilhard de Chardin was able to transcend the traditional dichotomies with a new dialectic, to reveal to us the living throbbing unity of the universe" (1966: 3).

In the *Phenomenon of Man* Teilhard describes the situation of modern scientists who are "now beginning to realise that even the most objective of their observations are steeped in the conventions they adopted at the outset and by forms or habits of thought developed in the course of the growth of research ... at the same time they realise that as the result of their discoveries, they are caught body and soul to the network of relationships they thought to cast upon things from outside: in fact they are caught in their own net ... Object and subject marry and mutually transform each other in the act of knowledge; and from now on man willy nilly finds his own image stamped on all he looks at" (1959: 32).

This does not however mean that we are locked up in our own subjectivity so that true knowledge is impossible. Teilhard believes that the human viewpoint on reality is uniquely privileged. Our subjective viewpoint happens to coincide with the centrepoint of the way things are in fact arranged so that we see them as they are. "It is peculiar to man to occupy a position in nature at which the convergent lines are not only visual but structural ... By virtue of the quality and the biological properties of thought, we find ourselves situated at a singular point, at a ganglion which commands the whole fraction of the cosmos that is at present within reach of our experience. Man, the centre of perspective, is at the same time the centre of construction of the universe. And by expediency no less than by necessity, all science must be referred back to him" (1959: 33).

The foundation of Teilhard's work, for Senghor, was his overcoming of dualism and materialism through his theory of a single basic energy with two complementary aspects, both involved to a greater or lesser degree in every event in world process. "On the basis then of the new discoveries, Teilhard de Chardin transcends the old dualism of the philosophers and the scientists, which Marx and Engels had perpetuated by giving matter precedence over the spirit. He advanced the theory that the stuff of the universe is not composed of two realities, but of a single reality in the shape of two phenomena; that there is not matter and energy, not even matter and spirit, but spirit-matter, just as there is space-time. Matter and spirit become a 'network of relations', as the French philosopher, Bachelard, called it: energy, defined as a network of forces. In matter-spirit there is, therefore, only one energy, which has two aspects" (1966: 3).

Teilhard called these two aspects of energy "radial" and "tangential" energy. These aspects are derived by him from analysing the process he calls "complexification". This is the process whereby over vast periods of time and through the effect of the interplay of large numbers, reality becomes more complex: basic elements are organised into atoms, which combine to become molecules, mega-molecules eventually being organised into cells, and so on through the ever increasing forms of biological life. For this process to occur there must be two distinct forms of energy, one of which is the principle of organisation within the unit, the other of which is the principle of interaction between units. The energy that organises, giving the organism a unity and centre, a "within", Teilhard calls radial, visualising the organism as a sphere. The energy that merely relates and connects things to each other in a sheer aggregated plurality he calls tangential. Of the two the radial is the more fundamental, since the direction of world process is towards ever greater complexification and hence "centreity"; both are nevertheless necessary. In Teilhard's own words "essentially, all energy is psychic in nature; but add that in each particular element this fundamental energy is divided into two distinct components: a tangential energy which links the element with all others of the same order (that is to say, of the same complexity and the same centricity) as itself in the universe; and a radial energy which draws it towards ever greater complexity and centricity – in other words forwards" (1959: 64).

The notion that all energy is fundamentally "psychic" sounds very odd, but becomes more intelligible when other aspects of Teilhard's thought are taken into account, in particular the connection he postulates between complexity and consciousness in his so-called 'Law of Complexity-Consciousness'. According to this law, the more complex, the more organised, a thing is, the more "centred" it will be, (the more distinct will be its "within"), and hence, beyond a certain level of complexity, the more conscious. Thus, from the beginning, the energy of the universe contains within it "psychic" potential. In Teilhard's words, "The degree of concentration of a consciousness varies in inverse ratio to the simplicity of the material compound lined by it ... Spiritual perfection (or conscious 'centreity') and material synthesis (or complexity) are but the two aspects or connected parts of one and the same phenomenon" (1959: 60).

It is not difficult to see the way in which Teilhard's theory of all energy being in the last resort "psychic" could be used to articulate the traditional African idea of force. Senghor uses it precisely for this purpose, delighted to find a scientific and philosophical vindication of his anti-materialist position. One has to admit that the parallels between Teilhard's system and the world-view of traditional African thought are in this respect striking.

One of the consequences of this unified metaphysical vision which is most apt for Senghor's purpose of systematising traditional African ideas, is the complete unity between humankind and the rest of the world that it entails. Everything that eventually appears in human nature is present in a less developed form throughout the universe; in the course of evolution the elements combine and a unique combination is produced. But there is no break in the web of relationships of force that combine to produce humanity out of simpler forms of life, and continue to support and develop human life into the ever new social forms it takes in the future.

There is another consequence of the law of complexity-consciousness which fits in well with Senghor's ultimate aim in constructing his system of negritude. This is the fact of there being a direction, and hence a centre, to world-process and evolution. The direction is towards ever greater complexity of organisation, and therefore towards ever greater "centering" and unity. This accounts for the special position of humankind, and the reason why our perspective on the world is a privileged one: we are the centre of the process, humanity is simply evolution become conscious of itself. In Teilhard's words the law of complexity-consciousness is one "that itself implies a psychically convergent structure and curvature of the world" (1959: 61).

This complexifying and centering continues even after the production of humanity, in human culture and labour and the construction of ever new forms of civilisation and society. This is the realm of what Teilhard calls the noosphere. Again this aspect of Teilhard's thought fits Senghor's purpose well. Summarising Teilhard, he writes, "But what is socialization-civilization? It is, the scientist answers, the organization of human relations, the re-construction of the earth – of nature, Marx and Engels would say – for the promotion of a new *human* society. By 'human society' we mean not one nation, one race, one continent, but all men without exception in a common effort of organization and reconstruction, of co-reflection" (1965: 137). Teilhard's theory of convergence is the perfect foundation for Senghor's idea of the "civilisation of the universal" and the "psychic miscegenation" that goes with it. The "human tendency to merge", as Senghor puts it, to synthesize their cultural products, is the conceptual foundation for the idea of the complementarity of cultures which is such an important element in negritude.

Finally there is the moral element, the element of human value in the whole Teilhardian scheme. The complexifying and centering goes on, as has been said, even once the human level has been reached. But here the radial energy that is its principal dynamism wears a truly personal face; it is the energy we know as love. Teilhard defines love as energy by taking the Thomist definition (the affinity of being with being) and re-expressing it in terms of his evolutionary world-view. "Love in all its subtleties is nothing more, and nothing less, than the more or less direct trace marked on the heart of the element by the psychical convergence of the universe upon itself" (1959: 265).

The importance of love as an energy of socialisation, for Teilhard, is that it is the only moral force that is capable of "personalizing" the developing order. We have not space here to spell out fully why Teilhard thinks this is so. A couple of quotations, by way of illuminating this crucial point, must suffice. "Love alone is capable of uniting living beings in such a way as to complete and fulfill them, for it alone takes them and joins them by what is deepest in themselves. This is a fact of daily experience. At what moment do lovers come into the most complete possession of themselves if not when they say they are lost in each other? In truth, does not love every instant achieve all around us, in the couple or the team, the magic feat, the feat reputed to be contradictory, of 'personalising' by totalising? And if that is what it can achieve daily on a small scale, why should it not repeat this one day on world-wide dimensions?" (1959: 265)

This phenomenon finds its explanation in a general principle of Teilhardian biology: union differentiates. "In any domain – whether it be the cells of a body, the members of a society or the elements of a spiritual synthesis – *union differentiates*. In every organised whole, the parts perfect themselves and fulfill themselves. Through neglect of this universal rule many a system of pantheism has led us astray to the cult of a great All in which individuals were supposed to be merged like a drop in the ocean or like a dissolving grain of salt. Applied to the case of the summation of consciousnesses, the law of union rids us of this perilous and recurrent illusion. No, following the confluent orbits of their centres, the grains of consciousness do not tend to lose their outlines and blend, but, on the contrary, to accentuate the depth and incommunicability of their egos. The more 'other' they become in conjunction, the more they find themselves as 'self'"(1959: 262).

When the union in question is a strictly personal one then it can only be achieved by means of love. "For the human particles to become really personalised under the creative influence of union – according to the preceding analysis – not every kind of union will do. Since it is a question of achieving a synthesis of centres, it is centre to centre that they must make contact and not otherwise. Thus, amongst the various forms of psychic interactivity animating the noosphere, the energies we must identify, harness and develop before all others are those of an 'intercentric' nature, if we want to give effective help to the progress of evolution in ourselves. Which brings us to the problem of love" (1959: 263).

Clearly this way of thinking is very sympathetic to what we have seen of traditional African thought and Senghor's understanding of it. Senghor's idea of "love-in-union" in particular seems to be a derivative of Teilhard's. Senghor uses it in an explicitly political context to define the conditions of a truly human society. As such it is the basis of his criticism of all other social systems. "Although all present political regimes – democracy, socialism, Communism – have as their goal totalization and socialization without depersonalization, they fail in the attempt. This is because they sacrifice the part to the whole, the person to the collectivity. Since a materialist postulate underlies this, and since the collectivity is conceived solely as a technical organization, it does not attract; to push the individuals towards it, one must resort to constraint and violence. This is the reason for the failures. But if one conceives of the collectivity as human convergence cemented by liberty, equality, fraternity – terms that Marx scorned – and if one places love of the Super-Person above human love, there will naturally be a powerful attraction to group individuals without constraint. For, once again, 'union differentiates', love personalizes" (1965: 147).

We have come to the end of our consideration of the way in which Senghor uses the thought of Teilhard de Chardin to express the insights of traditional

African thought in his system of negritude. I have said that it is a model for what I have attempted to do in the present study. Perhaps that was not quite accurate. I should have said it was the inspiration. Senghor's use of Teilhard, though copious and acknowledged, is not really systematic. Negritude appears as a collection of insights, each bearing a certain relation to the others deriving from their common origin, rather than as a systematic philosophy embracing a metaphysics, an ethics and a theory of the human person. Senghor is content to use Teilhard's concepts; he does not develop them or shape them in his own way. In spite of that I find his attempt impressive. He sees what needs to be done, and he gives us an example of how European and African thought can come together. In addition to that there is, I think, substantial truth in what he has produced, and he has applied his thought creatively to tackle the problems of post-colonial Africa.

I now propose to take a closer look at contemporary European culture and philosophy in order to offer my own diagnosis of what I regard as a critical inadequacy in the dominant philosophical conceptions of human nature and, indeed, of philosophy itself. Against that background I offer as an alternative a recent development of the Thomist tradition. It is this tradition of European philosophy which, to my mind, holds out a real possibility of a creative integration of European and African ideas.

Chapter Four

Contemporary Philosophy in Crisis

There is a tendency for the successful practice of science to produce its own ideology. Scientific knowledge is both so imaginatively stimulating and potentially useful that it is not difficult to understand the way in which it has come to be the paradigm of all knowledge worthy of the name. The sum of all the special sciences can, in a scientific culture such as ours, seem to constitute all possible knowledge. If there is anything that escapes the net thrown by science then it is not something we can in principle know anything about. This attitude gives rise to its own myth, a total picture of the universe and all that we can hope or do. The myth includes a view of reality in both macroscopic and microscopic terms: the ultimate framework of reality in space and time, and the ultimate elements that constitute each real thing and determine how it acts. As such it also provides a vision of all that we can reasonably hope or do. The gap between the microscopic limit of physics and the macroscopic framework of cosmology is filled in by all the detail of the other sciences, the natural, the biological and even the human, to increase the imaginative power of the picture and make it more immediately relevant to our own lives. Admittedly the picture is not yet complete but its main outlines are clear enough and quite sufficient to determine a way of life and a set of values. As it is added to we can expect to get a still clearer idea of our own deepest needs and how to satisfy them.

This is the myth, and as a myth it has the makings of greatness. It is however unsatisfactory, even as a myth, because it fails to include something essential. And it fails to include this because the science on which it is based fails to do so. And science can't include this missing something in its scope, not merely because it is insufficiently developed but because it is in principle incapable of doing so. Nevertheless what has been excluded is real and can be really known. I am thinking of the person of the scientist himself.

The nature of philosophy

When I speak of the person of the scientist I am thinking of the scientist as the one who knowingly and deliberately produces science, and with it the scientific picture of the world. I am thinking of the scientist as a thinking and choosing human subject, that is as an agent.

Of course science deals with human beings. There are the human sciences after all, as well as the current attempts to reduce the behavioural to the biological and even to the natural sciences. And contemporary cosmology and physics even take into account the position of the observer and the influence their observations have on the object of their study. But no science deals with (nor is fit to deal with) the scientist precisely as the producer of science, the one who devises its methods, decides on its procedures and judges the success of its results. This normative activity that actually is science is always presupposed to the body of knowledge that it produces and is not included in it. The knowledge we have of human beings as the result of some or other science is quite different from the knowledge we have of the activity that produces that science, and hence of ourselves as the real source of that activity.

The activity is certainly real. So therefore is its source, which can thus never be reduced to something that could be adequately known by any science. To enquire after the necessary conditions for science is thus to enquire into the nature of persons, precisely as subjects and agents. This is an intellectual task for which science is not suited. It is in fact the proper task of philosophy. At least it is how contemporary Thomist philosophy (which is the philosophical tradition I am trying to connect with African thought) conceives its task. What follows is my account of a contemporary Thomist understanding of philosophy and philosophical method.

We have of course a kind of knowledge of ourselves as subjects and agents, the knowledge of acquaintance. We cannot do anything without experiencing our subjectivity and agency. But we can have the experience and miss the meaning; philosophy is the attempt to acquire a true understanding of this dimension of our lives. So philosophy is bound to be very different from science. Insight into the nature of thinking and deciding, and so into our own nature as agents, is not merely gaining an item of knowledge additional to those gained through the sciences. Thinking and deciding, and hence science too, are a unique kind of activity because of their normative nature. They originate the notions of, and are constituted by a reference to, the true and the real. As such they cannot properly be seen objectively as distinct processes going on within the universe, different in nature but on the same level as everything else. Unlike all the other processes, they contain and are constituted by a reference to reality as such, not only to the "whole" of (actual and conceivable) reality, but to the "status" of being real that real things have and unreal things do not.

And so they contain and are constituted by a reference to and demand for truth that is absolute and unconditional. It is for this reason that these activities, or the dimension that they form, are all-inclusive, embracing all the objects of all the sciences in their scope, providing the milieu or medium in which alone they can be known. In this our subjectivity is rather like the space-time framework provided by cosmology and the fundamental elements of physics, a framework and source for knowledge, but one that is even more fundamental and all-encompassing. In investigating the necessary conditions for knowledge, by trying to gain insight into the activity which produces it, we are investigating the necessary conditions for being real.

When philosophy goes to work in this way, seeking a true understanding of that activity that produces knowledge, it begins as theory of knowledge, analysing the essential elements in knowing and deducing the necessary conditions for knowing to occur. But knowledge is true insight into the real. So such an analysis reveals the essential elements of reality as well, namely what reality must be like for us to be able to know it. This is what we call metaphysics.

Producing knowledge is an activity, so insight into knowledge includes insight into the nature of activity as such. This means that we have to come to understand desire, intention, will, choice and decision as elements in agency. Such understanding will constitute the outline of an ethics.

This then is the proper product of philosophy: a metaphysics and an ethics, a general theory of the real and of the good based on an insight into the activity which at one and the same time both produces knowledge and makes us agents.

It is important to be clear about this last point. Philosophy as a theory of knowledge, which includes a metaphysics and an ethics, is also an understanding of our own nature as persons, namely as subjects and agents. In other words implicit in our insight into knowledge is an insight into the nature of persons, an insight that is different from any acquired by science and which could be acquired in no other way. Kant saw this very clearly when he wrote in his Lectures on Logic that "All the interests of reason can be expressed in these three questions: What can I know? What ought I to do? What may I hope? The first is the question of metaphysics, the second the question of ethics, the third the question of religion. They can however all be included in the question What is man?, since to answer that question is to implicitly answer the other three as well." (Buber, 1961: 149) Kant's point is that to answer the question What is man? is to discover the necessary conditions for knowing what is true, what is good and what is possible. They are realised in us.

Philosophy thus has a double aim, a true insight into knowledge that includes both metaphysics and ethics, and an understanding of ourselves as subjects and agents. And in both these aims it transcends the scope of science. Because it has a different aim it also has a different method. We must now say something about this.

Philosophy's method

If the aim of philosophy is to come to a true understanding of what it is to think and choose so as to establish the necessary conditions for thinking and choosing well (which is what enables us to know the real and do the good), then it must have a method that is fitted to this aim. Since its field of study is made up of activities that are immanent to the agent, its method will not involve observation. Instead what is needed is reflection – by the subject on their own mental acts. By reflection I do not mean a sort of internal as opposed to external observation; I am not speaking of introspection. Reflection is an intellectual as distinct from a sensible scrutiny. Experience and memory – of thinking and choosing – are certainly involved, but what one concentrates on are the elements of meaning that are part of these activities. So in the place of experiment one has analysis.

The actual objects of study in philosophy are thus the concepts and the logical connections that make up the element of meaning in our thinking and choosing. Actually philosophy can also study the concepts and logic embodied in any part of human life, but if it is to do this in a fully systematic way then it must relate these to the foundational concepts and logic of thought and choice, concepts like real and true and thing and cause, act, end, good. Metaphysics and ethics form the foundation of philosophy and everything else is only properly understood once its position has been plotted on an ethical and a metaphysical map.

This having been said it is necessary to add, since it is so often overlooked, that to develop a metaphysics and an ethics in this way is at the same time to produce a philosophical view of persons as subjects and agents, since it is persons in whom the necessary conditions for thinking and choosing actually exist. And this leads to another set of fundamental concepts such as self and mind, intellect and will, intend and choose and free.

Since thinking and choosing are exemplified in all we do or say there is a literally infinite field of examples for us to explore in order to understand them better. For this reason the philosophical understanding that constitutes, say, metaphysics, is never complete. Each society, each language, each culture will provide more and different examples that can enrich our understanding of what it is to know or choose and how to know and choose better.

Consider contemporary scientific and technological European culture for instance. In his book *Insight* Bernard Lonergan takes natural science and mathematics as examples of what knowing is, and through an exhaustive analysis of how scientists and mathematicians come to know what they know, builds a whole theory of knowledge, complete with metaphysics and ethics as well. No-one could have built a metaphysics and an ethics on precisely that foundation before the twentieth century since it did not yet exist. Yet the metaphysics that Lonergan produces is very much the same as that worked out by Aristotle in the fourth century BC and by Aquinas in the Middle Ages. The activity of thinking, and thinking badly or well, remains the same but it is exemplified in very different ways. Similarly, in the field of ethics, love, pride and justice, as well as the family, the state and religion, take very different forms, but all illustrate the fundamental activity of choosing, and choosing well or ill.

I have been at pains to point out that a Thomist understanding of philosophy's aims and method entails an investigation of our own nature as persons, that is as subjects and agents. In conclusion I want to re-emphasise and further explain this aspect of the matter.

Philosophy as intellectual psychoanalysis

I hope my account of philosophy has made it clear that philosophy does not consist of a body of doctrine that can be merely learnt and then applied. Nor does it consist of a method that can be applied in an objective way to a field that is other than oneself. To practise philosophy properly is to carry out a critical investigation of the intellectual foundations of one's own life and experience. And the proper practice of philosophy must eventually issue in judgments as to the truth or falsity of one's most basic beliefs and values, as well as judgments concerning the goodness or badness of one's character and behaviour and commitments. In other words doing philosophy will not only produce a system of beliefs about reality and values. It will also produce a change in oneself.

As far as one's basic beliefs about what is real and good are concerned, philosophy will aim at making one more conscious of them, at overcoming contradictions between them so that they come to form a coherent system, and finally of judging their truth. It will thus aim at producing a view of the world and a system of values that one is fully conscious of, that contains no contradictions and which is rationally justified. As far as the change in oneself is concerned, the successful practice of philosophy will produce a foundation on which genuine self-knowledge and self-affirmation can grow. An insight into reality, including our own human nature, as well as into values, provides one with an objective criterion for evaluating one's own habitually held beliefs and ones behaviour. Such an insight is the only solid foundation for personal growth and integration.

For this reason it is not fanciful to think of philosophy as involving a kind of intellectual psychoanalysis. I think that this is certainly how both Socrates and Plato saw it. It also includes a creative or constructive aspect that tends to system and comprehensiveness. But these two aspects are really different sides of the same coin. To be properly built, the system must be built from the material (critically analysed and evaluated to be sure) discovered by reflection.

The Thomist understanding of philosophy I have just described is of course controversial. The dominant approaches in contemporary European (and in this is included English, American and Communist) philosophy would not agree with it. Nevertheless, unless one believes that in philosophy just as much as in science the new is the true, the fact that a philosophical approach is rejected by the majority of contemporary philosophers is not a final argument against it. When considered in the perspective of the whole history of European philosophy, the Thomist understanding of philosophy that I am advocating can be seen to be both the dominant one and the most enduring. Nevertheless truth is not determined by majority vote. A philosophical position must stand on its own arguments. I shall not be arguing further for this one in this book.

The crisis in contemporary philosophy

I do however propose to offer an indication of the alternatives. I do this in order to explain what I see as something of a crisis in contemporary European philosophy, a crisis deriving from the influence of science we have just been discussing. But it is also necessary in order for me to clarify what I take to be the real problem in contemporary European philosophy, and indeed in European thought and culture generally as it spreads across the globe – the problem it creates for Africa, and South Africa, today.

The idolisation of science leads naturally to philosophical materialism. When the knowing and acting subject is forgotten, both as part of reality and as determining a true understanding of the nature of the real through its own intellectual activity, then one of two different fates will result for actual science. In the first case it will undergo an automatic up-grading of status. Scientific knowledge will be knowledge pure and simple, and the object of science will be reality as such. Because this object is what is observed (in some way or other) and recorded and measured (in some way or other) and able to be expressed mathematically, then reality is precisely what is susceptible of all these operations. The real is the observable and measurable, namely the material.

This realist and materialist bent of science is so strong that it persists even in the teeth of a more sophisticated understanding of actual science that has gradually become dominant in the scientific community, largely through the influence of contemporary philosophers of the Anglo-American analytical kind. One could call this alternative understanding of science idealist provided that one doesn't take this to be anti-materialist. It consists of two components.

The first is the relativism affirmed by the human sciences of any product of human activity, science and all other forms of so-called knowledge included, since all these social products are conditioned by a variety of cultural determinants.

The second is the purely abstract nature of mathematics and therefore of all strictly scientific objects and laws. Since what science is able to verify has this abstract character it can't be material, much less observable. Hence either it is the case that reality is like this, abstract and immaterial, or else science does not give knowledge of reality in the traditional sense of knowledge. Since the first option is absurd (here speaks the power of the myth) the second must be true.

Science thus gives us not knowledge but models which we can apply (if we want to) in a way that is useful, helping us both to predict what will happen and also to control it. In this way the idealistic view of science as an intellectual technique in no way need disturb a thorough-going practical materialism. The metaphysical gap between the practice of science and the technological control of nature continues to exist but since all the interest is practical that does not really matter. In any case one could not ask for more.

Science is thus seen either as the only genuine knowledge of a necessarily material reality or else as an intellectual epiphenomenon of our practical attempt to control this same material world. In either case from a philosophical point of view one is materialist.

Within this materialistic view of the world the character of philosophy and its task is variously conceived. In one conception philosophy has a purely critical task. This it carries out primarily in relation to science in the practice of linguistic hygiene. The concepts and methods of the special sciences are subjected to semantic and logical scrutiny. It has a similar task however in the field of action, here concerned with the critical analysis of ideas and arguments in moral and political discourse. Such critical work can have a practical effect in the change of consciousness on the part of individuals, or a change in ideologies and the social institutions with which they are associated. In this conception philosophy appears as the handmaid of science and politics, and not as a distinct source of facts and values in its own right. The philosopher plays the part of the skeptic who questions the claims to authority in the spheres both of theory and of practice.

The alternative conception of philosophy sees it as a science in its own right, the super-science of human nature and history combined. This is the Communist conception. Philosophy is seen as a body of doctrine derived from a scientific scrutiny of human history from a particular uniquely privileged viewpoint in the process. This body of knowledge about human nature and society is objective in the same way as science is but, unlike science, is in its fundamentals irreformable. Like scientific knowledge it can be recorded and learnt; unlike scientific knowledge it is certain. Unlike science it comprises the fields of both ethics and metaphysics in its scope, though without recognising their non-scientific character. Philosophy in this conception has an essentially constructive and foundational character. It is intended to edify and to change the lives of those who come to believe it. It has much in common with religious dogma as far as its assumed status and its tone is concerned.

These two different conceptions of philosophy are related to the two different understandings of science I have outlined above, though not in any simple way. Both pairs should be seen as ideal constructions derived in the Platonic manner, by derogation from my own conception. I am thinking of a real historical situation and real movements of thought. But I am using my own conception of philosophy in order to make sense of them, and the method of using contrasting pairs is a useful one for focussing the mind and considering alternatives.

Materialism or dualism?

The metaphysical materialism that characterises contemporary European philosophy can take different forms. This is especially evident if one considers two different conceptions of the human person it has produced. The first is the highly individualistic conception associated with liberal political thought and free-market economics. Each individual is rather like an atom, separate, autonomous and constrained only by alien forces imposed on it from without. Morality is seen as an essentially private matter; the purpose of social regulation is to prevent interference with one independent centre of activity by others. In this view there is virtually no such thing as a common human nature. Everyone is different; the only thing we have in common is the capacity to originate action, the negative freedom to choose. As such we can of course be the subject of rights, but these rights are not derived from our common human nature. Rather they are produced by agreement of all interested parties.

A second conception is collectivist in character. Humanity subsists primarily in the social whole rather than in a plurality of individuals. Insofar as individuals participate in the social whole they can acquire humanity. The humanity so acquired is always specified by whatever place a person occupies within the system of social institutions that make up society; there is no common humanity that transcends the whole realm of institutions as such. The social whole itself is conceived as a kind of organism. There is no question of a freedom of independence for its members. Freedom is the lack of constraint produced by co-operation in common life, the overcoming of all kinds of conflict. In this conception morality becomes the will of the powerful, the class or the party or the state. Laws exist to ensure that the will of the powerful expresses the will of the "people", but there are no real conceptual restraints on a tendency to totalitarian state control.

What makes both these conceptions of the human person materialistic is that both fail to recognise a dimension of persons that transcends the scope of scientific knowability. And what is scientifically knowable is material in the sense outlined above. For this reason they are led to deny the existence of a human nature common to all persons. For the first view, apart from biological constants, each individual is unique, each with their own nature. There is nothing specifically human beyond the biological realm that is common to all. For the second the human is opposed to the natural. It is what is produced from it. And because human culture is produced wholly from material nature, materiality constitutes its substance and material factors determine the essential character of human life. There is no sense in which the human transcends the material.

As I have indicated above these rather abstract metaphysical views have ethical and political implications and consequences. Such basic conceptions of what it is to be a person underlie our whole understanding of and approach to life. So materialism has capitalist and communist, liberal and totalitarian, forms which on the surface appear very different. Essentially however they are embodiments of the same mistaken understanding of what it is to be a person.

The only alternative to these forms of materialism recognised by most contemporary European philosophy is dualism, usually of a fairly radical ghost-in-the-machine kind. When I say that it is recognised I do not mean that it is recognised as true. It is recognised as the only logically conceivable, though false, alternative to materialism of the one kind or the other. As far as persons are concerned, the dualism conceived by contemporary European philosophy has them consisting of two distinct elements or even substances, a soul and a body or mind and matter. The dualism that is rejected is very much a descendant of Descartes separation of all reality into thinking substance and extended substance. Sometimes, as with him, the person is identified with the soul or mind and the body becomes merely the appearance or the instrument of a person.

Dualism of this kind does not do justice to the unity of meaning and movement in human thought and action, nor to the importance of the links that unite persons to their natural and cultural environments. It is however an attempt, though an inadequate one, to do justice to the transcendent dimension in human life, the freedom and creativity manifested in our judgments and our choices. We shall return to this topic later with a more detailed discussion in which my philosophical critique of materialism and dualism will be set out. It was necessary to mention dualism at this point however since it is my opinion that one of the main values of the philosophical study of African traditional thought is the discovery of a conception of human persons that is non-materialistic without being dualistic either.

The idolisation of science in contemporary European culture tends to produce philosophy that sees materialism or dualism as the only possible alternatives when it comes to understanding human persons. A study of traditional African thought can help us to see that this is wrong.

Chapter Five

Traditional African Thought

In this chapter I am going to consider just two aspects of traditional African thought, both of which seem to me to offer a corrective to the dominant views in contemporary European philosophy. In particular the aspects I have chosen embody a conception of human persons that is neither dualistic nor materialistic.

The first is the conception of a person enshrined in the proverb *umuntu ngumuntu ngabantu*. This is the Xhosa expression of a notion that is common to all African languages and traditional cultures. A person is a person through persons. I want to examine in some detail what is contained in this idea.

Secondly there is the concept of *seriti*. Again this is the Xhosa term for an idea that is universal in African traditional thought. It can be translated as force or energy. It in fact expresses the fundamental metaphysical notion in African traditional thought and can be, and is, used to explain the conception of persons and personal life expressed in *umuntu ngumuntu ngabantu*.

Persons in community

In analysing the notion of *umuntu ngumuntu ngabantu* one is concerned both with the peculiar interdependence of persons on others for the exercise, development and fulfilment of their powers that is recognised in African traditional thought, and also with the understanding of what it is to be a person that underlies this.

A point agreed on by virtually all writers on the topic is that persons are defined not by this or that natural property or set of properties but by the relationships between them and others. So, for instance, Menkiti: "in the African view it is the community which defines the person as person, not some isolated static quality of rationality, will or memory" (1979: 158). In European philosophy of whatever kind, the self is always envisaged as something "inside" a person, or at least as a kind of container of mental properties and powers. In African thought it is seen as "outside", subsisting in relationship to what is other, the natural and social environment. In fact the sharp distinction between self and world, a self that controls and changes the world and is in some sense "above" it, this distinction so characteristic of European philosophy, disappears. Self and world are united and intermingle in a web of reciprocal relations. According to Taylor we must envisage a "centrifugal selfhood ... interpermeating other selves in a relationship in which subject and object are no longer distinguishable." "I think, therefore I am" is replaced by "I participate, therefore I am" (1963: 41).

A result of this is a loss of the radical unicity of the person that is traditional in all forms of European philosophy. Apostel makes the point as follows: "Western thought considers the individual both as an integrated unity (indivisible), and as radically distinct from the external world. African personality is neither as distinct nor as unified. Man does only exist in virtue of his relations to external forces: cosmic and social ones. And the very fact that he exists only through his relations with the external world entails that he possesses many distinct internal centres of personality, determined by these various relations" (1981: 36).

Taylor also speaks of the different relatednesses of the soul and of the way in which they constitute its being: "The different relatednesses of the self, which in the West we speak of as faculties or compartments of the mind, are pictured as separate entities rather loosely held together, each having a different source and a different function" (1963: 51). The notion of *seriti* and the metaphysical framework it entails helps clarify this externality and multiplicity of the self. The crucial relations in which the self subsists and the person comes to be are of course those with other persons. It is these we must now consider by looking at the African conception of community.

The emphasis placed on community by African thought is perhaps its most central and all-pervasive characteristic. Of course an emphasis on community is typical of the thought of all pre-scientific cultures. It would appear though that even in this company the African emphasis is unique, if only by virtue of its greater intensity.

The African conception of community is so universally embodied in customs and institutions, each of which expresses some or other aspect of its meaning, that a proper treatment of it would entail a wealth of anthropological detail. I am not going to provide this. My interest is in one or two aspects of the whole conception that are relevant to the state both of contemporary European philosophy and of contemporary African culture and society and its problems. These aspects are also in my judgement of genuine philosophical interest in their own right as well.

African writers try various ways of bringing out the uniqueness of their conception of community – by which I mean the set of relations between persons that enable persons to exist and grow as persons. A common way is to distinguish it on the one hand from individualism and on the other from collectivism.

So Menkiti, for instance, distinguishes the African idea of community from the view that sees it simply as "the aggregated sum of individuals". Instead it is "a collectivity in the truest sense", namely one where there is "an organic dimension to the relationship between the component individuals". Individuals develop within this organism; it is not formed by the association of individuals. Indeed African thought "asserts an ontological independence to human society, and moves from society to individuals" rather than, in the manner of Western thought, "from individuals to society" (1979: 165–167).

Senghor, though agreeing with Menkiti's anti-individualist account, is not happy with his collectivist alternative. His chief concern is to distinguish the African view of community from all the best-known European ones, all of which he labels "collectivist" in a negatively critical sense. He especially wants to differentiate the African view from any form of communism or European socialism, speaking instead of a "community society", and coining the term "communalism" to express the African conception. It is, he holds, "a community-based society, communal, not collectivist. We are concerned here, not with a mere collection of individuals, but with people conspiring together, *con-spiring* in the basic Latin sense, united among themselves even to the very centre of their being" (1963: 16).

European collectivism, on the other hand, is theoretically infected by the individualism against which it is in reaction: "To return to the distinction between Negro-African and collectivist European society, I would say that the latter is an assembly of individuals. The collectivist society inevitably places the emphasis on the individual, on his original activity and his needs. In this respect the debate between 'to each according to his labour' and 'to each according to his needs' is significant. Negro-African society puts more stress on the group than on the individual, more on solidarity than on the activity and needs of the individual, more on the communion of persons than on their autonomy. Ours is a community society. This does not mean that it ignores the individual, or that collectivist society ignores solidarity, but the latter bases this solidarity on the activities of individuals, whereas the community society bases it on the general activity of the group" (1965: 93).

From Senghor's description it could appear that he, like Menkiti, sees the individual merely as a function of the community, but this would be a mistake. Time and again he struggles to describe the crucial feature that distinguishes African communalism from European collectivism in a way that safeguards the dignity and value of the individual. He speaks for instance of black society being "based both on the community and on the person and in which, because it was founded on dialogue and reciprocity, the group had priority over the individual without crushing him, but allowing him to blossom as a person" (1966: 5).

Mulago uses the term "participation" in a special sense to denote the way in which the individual is seen as belonging to the group in African thought: "Participation is the element of connection which unites different beings as beings, as substances, without confusing them. It is the pivot of relationships between members of the same community, the link which binds together individuals and groups, the ultimate meaning not only of the unity which is personal to each man (person) but of that unity in multiplicity, that totality, that concentric and harmonic unity of the visible and the invisible worlds" (1971: 145). None of these descriptions is completely clear. One gets the impression of writers who share the same experience, and even have basically the same concept, yet who lack a philosophical framework and language with which to define it. It may be that it is at this point that genuine philosophy (of whatever kind or origin) has a role to play. We shall return to this question later.

In the above quotations Senghor speaks both of "the general activity of the group" and of dialogue as a special kind of activity that both creates and expresses a community. It is, I think, useful to see conversation or dialogue as the ultimate purpose and typical activity of a community as understood in African thought, since this is a co-operative activity that is achieved simply by the presence of person to person rather than by them fulfilling any further function, as would be the case in some practical activity such as building a house. In this connection it is interesting to note the special value that attaches to the idea of consensus in African political thought. As Wiredu remarks, "A much commended trait of our traditional culture is its infinite capacity for the pursuit of consensus and reconciliation" (1977: 52). Busia illustrates this in his account of a traditional council meeting to discuss matters affecting the whole community. "So strong was the value of solidarity that the chief aim of the councillors was to reach unanimity, and they talked till this was achieved." And he adds that "some have singled out this feature of talking till unanimity was reached as the cardinal principle of African democracy" (1967: 28).

Perhaps the best model for human community as understood in African thought is the family. The family has no function outside itself. It is a means of growth for its members, and the interaction, the companionship and conversation, between the growing and fully grown members is also an end in itself. African society is famous for its notion of the "extended family" (now seriously threatened by the advancing tide of European culture in its present degraded form). And the extended family is capable of extension to include anyone, not only those related by blood, kinship or marriage. In the last resort humanity itself is conceived of as a family, a family which one joins at birth but does not leave by dying. Because of this no-one is a stranger. The world is our common home, the earth the property of all. Because human life only exists by being shared, all that is necessary for that life, for living and living well, is shared by the human family as a whole.

Before we conclude our consideration of the conception of persons and community embodied in the saying *umuntu ngumuntu ngabantu*, there is a final important detail to be added.

Because persons subsist only in the relationships that unite them to others, the character of persons changes as these relations change. In African thought this change is understood in a very radical way. It is persons themselves and as a whole that change. We are in fact under construction. As we grow older we become more, more of a person, more ourselves. "One does not just take on additional features, one also undergoes fundamental changes at the very core of one's being" (Menkiti,1979: 159). Growth is always a normative notion. In African thought however the growth of a person has not only a psychological meaning but an ethical one. As Menkiti puts it, "personhood is something at which individuals could fail" (1979: 159). To grow older is (other things being equal) to become more of a person and hence to become more worthy of reverence and respect. Hence the great respect accorded the aged in African society. In this context moral evil is of course something of a problem, a problem I do not intend to tackle here. It is sufficient to say that it is understood in a way that is entirely consistent with this framework: moral evil involves the real destruction of the personality of the guilty person. It is not merely the incurring of a conventional penalty.

The idea of personal growth as progressive incorporation into the community is given expression in every African society by successive stages of initiation ritual. The basic structure of these initiation processes is finely described by Taylor (1963: 85–108).

The notion that personhood consists in incorporation in the community so that it is in some sense in its gift, is so strong in African thought that there is some disagreement as to whether unborn children, as yet un-named, or dead people who have been forgotten by their descendants, the "nameless" dead, exist as persons at all. Menkiti holds that they are not considered to have full personal status (1979: 161), but other writers disagree (Setiloane, 1986: 17–20). It may be that religion plays a part in which side one takes; in a Christian context a person's "name" is never forgotten by God. The whole significance of naming for African thought is of course of great anthropological importance, but it does not add anything of philosophical importance to the points already made.

The attempt to give the African conception of community concrete shape in actual social and political institutions is often called African socialism. Attempts to distinguish this conceptually from European socialism on the one hand, and all forms of liberalism on the other, also throw some light on the distinctively African conception of community that underlies this ideology. Apostel, for instance, writes as follows: "African socialism rejects both European socialism and Western capitalism because both could (and the second necessarily must) produce a relationship between man and object, that is one of person with thing (not a meeting of forces), and because both could produce a society in which the individual is alienated from others. Not the will of the majority but the will of the community, should be realised; and even in a classless society African tradition is still afraid of solitude and closed individuality. The desire to avoid these evils, and on the other side the desire to realise the autonomy of the person, avoiding any fusion in the whole, is a reflection of the tension met in African art and expressed in African philosophy" (1981: 381). As I see it the task of philosophy in contemporary Africa is primarily to overcome this apparent contradiction at the conceptual level.

The universe – a field of force

We come now to a consideration of our second concept, that of *seriti*, force or energy. As I have said this is the notion that supplies the metaphysical foundation and framework for the conception of persons and community considered above. And here again all writers on African philosophy agree that this notion is the most fundamental in traditional African world-views. Undoubtedly the most powerful and comprehensive exposition of the idea is that of Tempels. Whether one agrees completely with the accuracy of the exposition or not it remains a reference point for all other treatments of the topic.

According to Tempels, wherever European philosophy would think of being or substance, traditional African thought thinks of force: "I believe that we should most faithfully render the Bantu thought in European language by saying that Bantu speak, act, live as if, for them, beings were forces. Force is not for them an adventitious, accidental reality. Force is even more than a necessary attribute of beings: force is the nature of being, force is being, being is force" (1959: 51).

There is a similarity between this idea of being and that of Aristotelian and Thomist philosophy. First of all, for Thomism, the most fundamental distinction within the notion of being is that between potency and act. Beings are real insofar as they are in act. So the best way to think of anything that exists is as something actively being itself; the closest equivalent to existence itself is activity.

The African concept of force certainly contains this idea of activity (and hence, one might add – though as far as I know, Tempels doesn't – the distinction between potency and actuality). But it also contains the idea of influence on another, of a movement or pressure "outwards", an active relationship to the rest of the universe of forces. The African idea of force has a global reference that is quite fundamental (a "field of forces") in a way that the European idea of being has not; beings are always somehow "self-contained".

Another similarity between the African idea of force and at least the Thomist idea of being is that both are strictly analogous notions. Neither term identifies a "kind" of reality, a "nature" or "essence", but rather that which makes the different natures or essences real. So force in African traditional thought cannot be identified with any particular kind of energy that science might discover, however fundamental. It is closer to the transcendental notion of energy itself that underlies and gives impetus to Western science.

So force is not something like a fundamental material of which everything is composed. Every different kind of thing is a kind of force, but this does not mean that they can be reduced to the same kind of thing. All differences are derived from the primordial sea of force.

This applies especially to the difference between material and spiritual, or psychic or mental, forces. This distinction though real is not fundamental. We shall see presently the importance of this when we come to consider the use of the idea of force in the sphere of human life.

We must now attempt a brief sketch of the view of the universe presented by African traditional thought in terms of the basic notion of force.

As I have already suggested, the basic picture is one of a universal field of force. The origin of all force and the origin of the universe is God. As such God is immanent in everything that exists, giving it existence at each moment that it exists, the source of all forces in their actual operation, and of their increase or decrease. As Tempels says, "It is He who has force, power, in himself. He gives existence, power of survival and of increase, to other forces" (1959: 61). This permanent causal relationship between God and the universe, whereby He keeps it in being and empowers it to act, is the model for the causal connections between everything in the universe as well. Tempel describes this important notion of causality well: "Bantu hold that created beings preserve a bond with one another, an intimate ontological relationship, comparable with the causal tie which binds creature and Creator. For the Bantu there is interaction of being with being, that is to say, of force with force. Transcending the mechanical, chemical and psychological interactions, they see a relationship of forces which we should call ontological. In the created force (a contingent being) the Bantu sees a causal action emanating from the very nature of that created force and influencing other forces" (1959: 58). As we shall see, this conception of causality has a most important function in the African understanding of human life and the relationships between persons.

There are two other features of this view of the universe that are of relevance to our interest in this article. These are its hierarchical structure and the fact that it is centred on humanity.

The hierarchy of the universe is a hierarchy of strength or power. God is at the top, inanimate things at the bottom, with humanity in the middle. It is moreover a dynamic system in that the force of everything, at least all living things, is continuously being either strengthened or weakened. Human beings continuously influence each other, either directly or indirectly by way of sub-human forces or through the ancestors. It must be remembered that when one speaks of humanity in the context of African thought one is not speaking only of the living. The dead play a very important part in the whole universe of forces, and continue to interact causally with the living.

In this universe humanity occupies the central place, and this is true not only in the sense that we occupy the middle tier of the hierarchy of force, but also in the sense that we are at the centre of the stage, the most important players in the drama. In a way that is akin to the traditional European conception of the *theatrum mundi* (the world as a stage for the human drama), humanity is "what the world is all about". We are the whole point of the plot, and even God plays a part that is ancillary to our own. The earth is our home and God would like to make it his own home too. But whether he can or not depends on us. He may be the author of the play, but it is a play about humanity; if he wants a part in it he must be obedient to its plot.

The power of persons

We come now to consider how this notion of force is deployed in the account given by African thought of human nature and human interaction and community. A vivid description by Setiloane corroborates Tempels' insistence that the African idea of force includes both the material and the spiritual elements of life: "the human person is like a live electric wire which is ever exuding force or energy in all directions. The force that is thus exuded is called *seriti. Seriti* has often been translated to mean dignity or personality. Actually, that only describes the end result of the phenomenon. It is derived from the same word-stem *-riti* as *moriti* which means 'shadow' or 'shade'. It is a physical phenomenon which expresses itself externally to the human body in a dynamic manner. It is like an aura around the human person, an invisible shadow or cloud or mist forming something like a magnetic or radar field. It gives forth into the traffic or weltering pool of life in community the uniqueness of each person and each object. While physically its seat is understood to be inside the human body, in the blood, its source is beyond and outside of the human physical body ..." (1986: 13).

Everything that has been said above regarding the nature of force and the hierarchical system of interacting forces that constitutes the universe, can be said again with regard to human life, and exemplified in the peculiar interdependence of persons on other persons that we have already discussed.

Seriti is the energy or power that both makes us ourselves and unites us in personal interaction with others. As Setiloane puts it, "*Seriti* is not neutral. Its very existence seems to be calculated to promote and participate in relationship with the external world, human, animal, animate, inanimate, and even spiritual, like an antenna, charged and sensitive" (1986: 14). Tempels expresses it even more explicitly: "Just as Bantu ontology is opposed to the European concept of individuated things, existing in themselves, separated from others, so Bantu psychology cannot conceive of man as an individual, as a force existing by itself and apart from its ontological relationships with other living beings and from its connection with animals or inanimate forces around it. The Bantu cannot be a lone being. It is not a good enough synonym for that to say that he is a social being. No; he feels and knows himself to be a vital force, at this very time to be in intimate and personal relationship with other forces acting above him and below him in the hierarchy of forces. He knows himself to be a vital force, even now influencing some forces and being influenced by others. The human being, apart from the ontological hierarchy and the interaction of forces, has no existence in the conceptions of the Bantu" (1959: 103).

It is difficult to say, in this perspective, which is the more fundamental, the self that develops in the interaction with others, or the influence of others that enables it to develop. The ontology of force allows one to see them as equiprimordial, since both are aspects of the same universal field of force. Here is Setiloane again, struggling to express this conception of a person in which the very status of personhood is derived from the relationship with others: "This manner of understanding human personality explains the interplay which takes place when people come into contact or live together. The essence of being is 'participation' in which humans are always interlocked with one another. The human being is not only 'vital force', but more: vital force in participation". The all-important principle is this "vital participation" which forms the very soul of the community body and accounts for the miasma which attaches to the group, the clan or the tribe. "'Participation' with its concomitant element of 'belonging' is made possible by *seriti*, which is ever engaged in interplay with other people's *diriti* whenever they come into contact" (1986: 14).

The picture that emerges from the above descriptions is the same as the one we encountered when considering the idea of persons and personal community embodied in the expression *umuntu ngumuntu ngabantu*. Persons appear to have no existence apart from their relations with other persons. At the level of common experience, the experience expressed by the proverb, this is paradoxical though it has the ring of truth. At the theoretical level, the level at which the notion of *seriti* is supposed to operate with explanatory power, it appears to be contradictory. If the self is constituted by its relations with others, what are the relations between? It is difficult to see how persons and personal relations can be equally primordial. Indeed in the perspective opened up by the African idea of the universe as a field of forces, it is difficult to see how the existing individual can have any enduring reality at all, much less how he can be possessed of the freedom and responsibility that is usually reckoned the most valuable mark of personhood.

That this is a real problem for African thought is emphasised by Apostel when he argues that the life-force metaphysics of African thought entails a plurality of personalities within the individual person, a plurality corresponding to the multiplicity of relationships in which he stands to his social and natural environment. In the last resort the real unity of the individual depends on the unity of the social milieu in which he lives. Apostel finds this a powerfully accurate picture of the actual state of affairs in African, and indeed in all human, society; it is a picture that defines the moral and political task of humanity. The world-view of African thought is true to life (1981: 36–37, 384–385). While this may be true as far as it goes, I do not think it goes far enough. A general account of social phenomena in terms of a key-concept such as *seriti* cannot claim to be philosophical unless it can be shown to be necessary in some sense. And this African traditional thought never attempts to do.

The writers we have referred to nevertheless clearly feel that it is something that in principle could be done. The experience of reciprocity and mutuality identified in *umuntu ngumuntu ngabantu* seems to fit in with the metaphysical vision focussed in the idea of *seriti*. If it doesn't fit in with the intuitions and the metaphysical assumptions of European philosophy then so much the worse for that. My feeling in this matter is not so much that all European philosophy of whatever kind is simply mistaken in this matter, but that the African understanding of persons and community hasn't quite reached the level of philosophy. An insight is there, and one that European philosophy has largely lost; but it is not philosophically articulated. I think it can be however, and will presently attempt to do so.

Thus far we have considered *seriti* as a broadly metaphysical notion, and its application as such to an understanding of human nature and community. But it also has an ethical dimension. As Tempels makes clear, "Objective morality to the Bantu is ontological, immanent and intrinsic morality" (1959: 121). The fundamental norm in the ethics of traditional African thought is human nature itself: "it is the living *muntu* who, by divine will, is the norm of either ontological or natural law" (1959: 121). And, as this nature is understood in terms of *seriti*, of vital force, so the moral life in all its individual, social and political ramifications is understood as the struggle to increase the power of this force. "The activating and final aim of all Bantu effort is only the intensification of vital force. To protect or to increase vital force, that is the motive and the profound meaning in all their practices. It is the ideal which animates the life of the *muntu*, the only thing for which he is ready to suffer and to sacrifice himself" (1959: 175). Anything that diminishes this force is evil, anything that increases it is good.

For this reason there is much more of a continuity between moral and physical evil than contemporary European thinking would admit. Of course in traditional African culture this understanding of good and evil is expressed in a variety of superstitious and magical practices. Contemporary African philosophers such as Wiredu are, unlike the anthropologists and other social scientists, extremely critical of traditional thought on this account. On the other hand the inextricable connection envisaged between the voluntary and the determined, the deliberate and the habitual, the will and the body, is a salutary corrective to the dualistic emphasis of European medicine and psychotherapy. When this dualism is resolved in European culture it is almost always in favour of the material, so that, for instance, drugs are widely used to treat psychological disorders. Here too traditional African thought is a corrective, looking always (and, it must be admitted, often in irrational and dangerous ways) for causes that are strictly personal.

A final remark on this idea of goodness as increase of vital force. It must be remembered that being and force are synonymous in this system of thought. So the force that comes to me to increase my vital force can't be seen as being merely added to me. Although it *comes* to me, it becomes my own vital activity. In receiving it I become more myself. To put it in a somewhat "European" idiom: it is a transformation from *within*. This is an intimation of something that I will stress when I attempt a more rigorous account of personal relations that also does justice to the African ideas.

Chapter Six

The Thomist Tradition

Our consideration of traditional African thought regarding the human person has revealed a very different conception of human persons from anything contained in the dominant schools of contemporary European philosophy. Our analysis of *umuntu ngumuntu ngabantu* has confronted us with an anti-individualist understanding of persons which nevertheless does not fit into any of the forms of European collectivism. And in analysing the notion of *seriti* we have uncovered a set of metaphysical ideas that are neither materialist nor dualist in the common European senses of those terms. Is there a connection between the special African understanding of community, and a metaphysical account of persons that is neither materialist nor dualist? I think there is. I also think that this connection is the clue to an adequate philosophical understanding of persons, and hence too to a solution to the intellectual (and ideological) conflicts that bedevil contemporary Africa.

It is against this background that I propose to attempt to answer the two questions regarding the relation between Africa and philosophy that I posed above. Can traditional African thought be of help to contemporary philosophy? And can philosophy be of help to contemporary African thought? I think the answer to both these questions is "Yes". African thought presents us with a conception of persons and human community that is a much needed corrective to those in the dominant European philosophies, which underlie the competing political ideologies in Africa at the moment. This conception is not, it is true, philosophically articulated, but it is one that is big with philosophical import and suggestiveness. It could serve as the inspiration for a strictly philosophical elaboration of the elements it comprises. A systematic philosophical account of the nature of persons and community would moreover, in my view, be the greatest gift philosophy could give to contemporary Africa in the intellectual (and not only intellectual) predicament in which it finds itself at present.

The rest of this book will consist mainly of my attempt to provide at least in outline such a systematic account, that avoids both materialism and dualism, and which is centred on the African insight embodied in *umuntu ngumuntu ngabantu*. In so doing I will be supplying my own answer to the two questions I have raised, an answer to which our consideration of traditional African thought has provided the crucial clue.

In what follows I will of course be drawing on my own philosophical background which, like that of most philosophers in Africa, is European. In spite of my critical stance towards the dominant forms of contemporary European philosophy I by no means reject the whole tradition of European philosophy. More than any other it contains its own self-critical vitality. And there are (less influential) schools of contemporary European philosophy that are sensitive to the issues that I have raised. In particular I will be drawing on the work of contemporary Thomist philosophers as well as recent writers in the personalist and phenomenological traditions of philosophy.

In what I am doing I have a model, namely Leopold Senghor. He saw in the tradition of French philosophy emanating from Bergson, and especially in the multidisciplinary writing of Teilhard de Chardin, a philosophical vehicle for conveying the distinctive insights of traditional African thought. Nor did he limit himself to these French thinkers but drew on the work of Marxian and existentialist philosophers too. In many ways his criticism of contemporary European philosophy is the same as mine. But he escaped infection by the ideology of scientism and used his own background in European philosophy to understand and to express the insights of his African ancestors.

In order to put my own attempt into perspective I need to say something about the philosophical background on which I draw.

There are two traditions of thought regarding the human person in European philosophy from which I want especially to draw, an older going back at least as far as Plato, and a more recent, going back only to Hegel as far as I can see.

Persons are spiritual

The older view is that which sees human nature as defined by its possession of rationality or mind. The human being is – as, for instance, for Aristotle –

a rational animal. Such a definition (by genus and species) does itself suggest a certain duality in the thing defined. This duality was intensified by the way in which Plato and, following him, the whole tradition of Greek thought, understood our rationality.

The concepts that our minds deal with and which make up all our knowledge are, unlike the images provided by our senses, universal in character. The concept "human", for instance, can be applied equally to all human beings whatever their particular characteristics. It is not itself particular in any way. Since our minds are capable of handling and understanding such concepts they too cannot be particular in any way, for then their particularity would disturb or destroy the generality of the concepts they were using. But all material things of the kind that our senses and imaginations can know are particular (that is have a particular colour, position, weight and so on). Hence our minds cannot be material.

This way of thinking led to the affirmation of a distinction between an immaterial mind and a material body in every human being. With that, dualism was introduced into European philosophy and reigned throughout the Middle Ages.

Such dualism was at odds with biblical – and so with Christian – thought, which stressed the radical unity of the human person as the 'image of God'. Aquinas therefore set himself the task of reconciling the biblical understanding of persons with Greek philosophical categories. He used the newly rediscovered writings of Aristotle to do this, in the famous "hylomorphic" theory of human nature. In human beings mind and matter are related as form to matter. For Aristotle, in opposition to Plato, form and matter were only distinct aspects of really existing things. They had no existence of their own outside the thing. Matter was that which distinguished a particular thing from other things, even from other things of the same kind; form was what gave the thing its identity or character as a real example of a certain class or category of thing. In human beings, Aquinas argued – following Aristotle – the mind is the form; its union with matter is the one living bodily being.

In spite of this apparent transcendence of dualism in the philosophy of Aquinas, the history and habit of dualistic thought in European philosophy proved too strong. Whenever the immateriality of the mind was affirmed a dualistic metaphysics was automatically implied. And this was merely intensified and radicalised after the advent of modern science. The mind and the body came to be seen – as in Descartes for instance – as simply different kinds of thing. In such a context the only alternative to substantial dualism, and the dualistic view of persons that goes with it, is some or other form of materialism.

The tradition of European philosophical reflection on the human person that we are presently considering can with some justice claim to be the central and most all-pervasive one. From Plato and Aristotle, through Augustine and Aquinas to Descartes and Kant, however different individual philosophers might have been, there is a remarkable consensus in their understanding of persons. And this has centred on the view that in some way or other persons transcend the material realm. Indeed, for this tradition it is precisely this transcendence that is signified when human beings are called, in the technical sense, persons. It is the source of everything that has come to be associated with the notion of persons in European thought: moral responsibility, dignity, freedom of choice, agency and even immortality. It is the source too of the idea that persons are the subjects of duties and rights that go far beyond those that may be granted or imposed on them by any particular state or legal system.

This insight is one I wish to preserve in the outline I propose to give, but I wish to preserve it in a form detached as far as possible from any dualistic misconception. It is in this context that the work of the contemporary Thomist Karl Rahner has proved so valuable.

The relational view of persons

In spite of the Aquinas' attempt at synthesis, the dualist potential of the older conception of persons was revivified in the centuries that followed Aquinas. As I have already pointed out, this philosophical development was intensified by that of the natural sciences at this period. The methods of the natural sciences fostered a conception of nature as a mechanical, or at any rate a physical, system. The notion of physical extension, *partes extra partes*, as also that of measurable regular forces producing changes in the position and behaviour of otherwise inert substances, was diametrically opposed to the notion of persons that had developed during the Middle Ages. Even the atomism built into the scientific conception, though superficially similar to the radical individuality of persons, was in fact the very antithesis of it. Whereas each person was a unique origin of life and activity, each atom was merely an identical unit of a homogeneous flux. The extreme dualism of

Descartes was a perhaps inevitable result of this vision of the natural world. Human persons were after all thinking subjects and as such quite distinct from the objects of their (scientific) thought. At the same time there could be no doubt that our bodies are part of the same objectified world studied by science. A dualism of substance seemed a necessity for reflective thought.

Such a dualism of substance fitted ill with the theoretical superstructure of the natural sciences. The predominance of the notion of matter in the natural sciences led ineluctably to metaphysical materialism. The success and prestige of natural science saw a generalisation of its object and method to encompass the whole of reality. So even where a dualist theory of human nature was maintained, it was against the background of a naively realist theory of science that had an internal affinity with materialism. Human nature appeared as a glaring exception in an otherwise admirably unified picture of reality.

During the nineteenth century, however, a reaction to dualism began that had quite distinctive features of its own. There is, firstly, the development of the human as distinct from the natural sciences. In all sorts of ways human behaviour begins to be explained in the same way as things are explained in the natural sciences, namely as the result of external influences from the environment. Now however it is primarily the social and cultural environment that is seen as the source of explanation. This new approach to the understanding of human nature is of course typically exemplified by Marx. It is taken even further by Darwin to include influences from the natural environment as well.

Our dependence on our environment, both natural and social, is what makes us fit objects for scientific study. The examination of such causal relations between us and our environment is the common method of all the human sciences, from psychology to history. But at this period it also becomes the object of an explicitly philosophical interest, beginning with the work of Hegel.

The idea that the person, the self, the human "I", is the product of, or the creature of, environmental forces and social relationships, roles, functions and meanings, is the crucial philosophical element in the human sciences. Its first appearance, as far as I know, is, fittingly enough, in Hegel's *Phenomenology*. Here the distinctively human individual gains its being and realises itself only in relation to what is other than itself, especially in relation to the social milieu of other human persons. "Self-consciousness exists in itself and for itself, in that, and by the fact that it exists for another self-consciousness; that is to say, it *is* only by being acknowledged or 'recognised'" (1910: 229). This is Hegel's ultra-abstract way of formulating the basic methodological presupposition of the social sciences.

Hegel quite explicitly set himself the philosophical task of overcoming the dualistic understanding of human nature that found such powerful expression in the philosophy of Kant. What is new in his alternative to dualism is that it is also a rejection of mechanism of any sort and the atomism that this entails. Charles Taylor brings this out very well in his study on Hegel. He writes, "Hegel is in fact one of the important links in a chain of thought in modern philosophical anthropology, one which is opposed to both dualism and mechanism, and which we see continued in different ways in Marxism and modern phenomenology" (1975: 80).

Hegel is determined to do justice to what he saw as the truth in the spiritual understanding of persons that had ruled from Plato to Aquinas, but without being a dualist. This is not the place to provide my own interpretation of Hegel's understanding of human nature as "Spirit". It has been very variously interpreted and the debate continues. But there can be little doubt that the notion lives on most influentially in Marxism, and in existentialism and phenomenology. What these schools of thought have in common is what they have inherited from Hegel. And, in a nutshell it is this: humanity is not a natural essence but a historical product. Put otherwise, human nature is what our particular biological species has created by virtue of its transformation of nature as such.

Humanity is thus self-creating and, as such, is essentially a social and cultural entity. Individuals gain their humanity by virtue of their participation in the common social and cultural world that precedes them, they do not have it by a natural necessity. So Marx: "The individual *is* the social being... In his species-consciousness man confirms his real social life, and reproduces his real existence in thought; while conversely, species-life confirms itself in species-consciousness and exists for itself in its universality as a thinking being" (Fromm,1961: 130). And Heidegger: "*Dasein* is essentially *Being with ... Being with* is an essential characteristic of *Dasein* even when factically no Other is present-at-hand or perceived. Even *Dasein's Being-alone* is *Being-with* in the world" (1962: 137).

The move from metaphysics

The new language reveals a new world of thought. For Hegel (or Marx or Sartre) to say that humanity is a social being is to say something very different from what Aristotle would have meant by the term. For Aristotle (and Aquinas) a human being's sociality was part of his inherited nature, bound up with the capacity for reason and speech. For Hegel and the philosophical tradition emanating from him it is rather to identify the social and cultural world as the distinctively human thing, in contradistinction to everything merely natural. In fact the distinctively human is not a thing at all in the ordinary sense of thing; the world of nature and the human world are utterly different conceptions, the objects of two utterly different points of view.

The difference I am indicating here is an ontological difference. In the last resort human realities are only cultural realities, and thus ontologically less fundamental than the realities dealt with by the natural sciences. What has happened in the history of philosophy from Hegel to existentialism and Marxism is a movement away from the metaphysical to the phenomenological; the analyses of human phenomena supplied by the philosophers in this tradition are in most cases accounts of how things are experienced rather than how things really are. Sometimes, of course, there is the unspoken conviction that this is how things *must* be experienced, but usually there is the opposite assumption, that the way things are experienced depends largely on the person's social and cultural situation.

For this reason the new non-dualist account of human nature given by Hegel did not mean a victory over metaphysical materialism after all. It simply initiated a shift away from metaphysics to phenomenology and to science, science now seen not as knowledge of reality but as the production of useful models for prediction and control. Insofar as the question was ever raised, it was simply assumed that materialism was true; there was no *distinctively* spiritual reality transcending the realm of the sensible and measurable. A generally materialistic world-view continued to prevail, though with its status as useful knowledge denied it, at least by Marxists and phenomenologists and the more sophisticated philosophers of science.

So Hegel's attempt to preserve the classical insight into the nature of persons as rational and therefore spiritual beings failed. The non-dualistic form he gave it nevertheless succeeded beyond even his grandiose expectations. He succeeded in giving a philosophical formulation of the basic principle underlying all the human sciences, namely our dependence on our social and cultural milieu for everything we are and do. I call this the relational view of persons, since it is not concerned with any supposed common nature present in each human individual but in the particular set of causal relations that makes each individual what they are.

With this methodological presupposition the human sciences have vastly increased our understanding of human behaviour and society. At the properly philosophical level too we find a form of philosophy that has really learnt from science, namely phenomenology. It is rooted in the world revealed by science, especially the human sciences, but exercises a critical and systematic function the sciences themselves are incapable of. At its best it recognises the partiality of the sciences, not merely the partiality of each science vis-a-vis the others, but the partiality of science itself, as but one among other modes of knowledge of the human subject, and deliberately seeks to go beyond it as all good philosophy should. When phenomenology exhibits this character it produces descriptions of *necessary* features of the relations that bind the knowing and acting subject to the world, features that precede and include everything the sciences can discover. The necessity asserted in these accounts indicates that the features in question are not *merely* subjective, but have a claim to ontological status.

Phenomenological philosophy preserves the Hegelian insight insofar as its object of study is always the person-in-relation to the world, modes of being-in-the-world or structures of existence (*ek-sistere*). Among philosophers in this tradition a number have concentrated their work especially on that dependence of persons on relations with other persons for their own development that is such a central motif of traditional African thought (Buber, 1958; Feldstein, 1976; Heidegger, 1962; Heron, 1970; Macmurray, 1959; Merleau-Ponty, 1964; Scheler, 1973; Strasser, 1969; Ver Eecke, 1975).

I want to preserve what I see as the truth of the relational view of persons, as originated by Hegel and elaborated by these later authors, but without the materialism that always threatens phenomenology in a scientific culture.

Contemporary Thomism

I wish now to take a look at how contemporary philosophers in the Thomist tradition have attempted to preserve and even to combine the two traditions regarding the nature of persons I have discussed above. First I will give an account of Karl Rahner's work in this area since he tackles the issue in an explicitly metaphysical way. Then I will refer to the work of writers in the Thomist tradition who attempt to provide phenomenological descriptions of the phenomena of the intersubjective relations of persons that fit the metaphysical categories developed by writers such as Rahner. I intend to use both in my own attempt to present a summary but systematic account of persons and community that incorporates the African insights and is suitable for African use.

Rahner follows Aquinas in recognising our intellectual capacities as those that make us in the technical sense persons. But he expresses the immateriality of the intellect and its activity in a novel way, though one that has its origins in Aquinas. (The works of Rahner especially important for understanding his philosophical anthropology are the following: *Hominisation*, 1965; *Spirit in the World*, 1968; *Hearers of the Word*, 1969; *Foundations of Christian Faith*, 1978. For an excellent discussion of Rahner's anthropology that extends also to the specifically theological essays in his *Theological Investigations* (a multi-volume series of theological writings) one should refer to Andrew Tallon's *Personal Becoming*, 1982. This book also includes an exhaustive bibliography of works by or about Rahner.

The immateriality of the intellect consists in its reflexivity, the fact that it is able to be aware of and act upon itself. "Being a person, then, means the self-possession of a subject as such in a conscious and free relationship to the totality of itself" (Rahner, 1978: 30). This *reditio in seipsum* (turning back on oneself) revealed in the peculiarly radical self-awareness and self-determination of persons, could not be a characteristic of anything material since it involves the presence of the intellect, as a whole, to the whole of itself, not of one part to another as, for instance, in a self-scanning computer. This capacity of the intellect to be present to itself and act upon itself thus shows that it is simple, in the technical sense of having no co-existing parts, and so immaterial. The *locus classicus* for this idea in Aquinas is *Summa Contra Gentiles, IV, 11*. Commenting on this passage Rahner writes, "In this perfect return to itself St. Thomas sees the distinctive attribute of the spirit in contrast to all that is sub-spiritual" (1969: 54).

Rahner has his own explanation of how such cognitive and volitional self-possession entails the simplicity and universality (and hence immateriality) of the mind which make it different from anything material, which of necessity is always particular or "finite": "a finite system of individual, distinguishable elements cannot have the kind of relationship to itself which man has to himself ... A finite system cannot confront itself in its totality. From its point of departure, which is ultimately imposed upon it, a finite system receives a relationship to a definite operation, although this might consist in maintaining the system itself, but it does not have a relationship to its own point of departure" (1978: 29). The simplicity of the mind that defines it as spiritual is thus not of a monadic kind, such as that of an indivisible fundamental particle of the kind postulated by modern physics. Instead it is the unique feature of that presence-to-self and self-determination characteristic of the life of persons.

Like Aquinas, Rahner deduces the fact of human spirituality from his analysis of our capacity for knowledge. He also performs a similar deduction to show that it is a necessary condition for deliberate decision and action. In both these spheres of human life this self-referential character of persons results in our transcendence of our own particularity and its limitations to a certain degree. In knowledge we are able to enter into the being and grasp the nature of what is other than our own minds. And in our deliberate acts we are self-determining in a way that transcends the limiting influences that external causes have on our own will.

In spite of placing such emphasis on the spirituality of persons, Rahner is true to the Thomist tradition in insisting that as far as human persons are concerned, our most spiritual activity is impossible without our materiality, our body. Rahner in fact prefers to speak of our spirituality and our materiality rather than our soul and body, since he is concerned to avoid Cartesian overtones, and to emphasise the radical unity of the human person. Indeed he is at great pains to show how the material elements in, for instance, knowledge, such as sensation and imagination, are expressions or manifestations of the purely intellectual ones. The body itself he understands as the manifestation, the symbol, of spirit. So there is no thought, however abstract, without images, and therefore sensations. There is no act of the will, however pure, that is without emotion, and therefore inclination.

In trying to describe the experienced duality of human life in a way that does not lapse into a dualism of substance or even a dualism of parts, Rahner prefers to use the language of relations. Human persons are constituted by a duality of relations. There is the peculiar relation-to-self (self-consciousness, self-determination), and this is what constitutes our spirituality. And then there is the relation of dependence on what is other than oneself (manifested in all our sensations and inclinations), and this constitutes our materiality.

What is called the body is the real relation to, and dependence on, otherness that characterises human persons. What is called the soul is the peculiar constitutive relation that persons have to themselves, and which defines them as persons. The paradoxical feature of human life is that the enactment of the one relation is impossible without the other. It is paradoxical since the one relation is what makes us free and self-determining, whereas the other is that of our dependence on things other than ourselves.

The idea that a person is defined by a relation to themselves is perhaps strange. I hope to give it more content in what is to follow. The relation to what is other that defines human materiality is given content by the work of the Thomist phenomenological philosophers I have referred to. Writers such as Donceel (1967), Johann (1966; 1975; 1976), Luijpen (1960), Nedoncelle (1966), Toner (1968) and others, all offer accounts of the fundamental relationships between persons that confirm the spirituality of persons on the Rahnerian model. In particular they highlight in different ways certain peculiar features of the intersubjective relations between persons that could only be accounted for if persons were the self-reflexive beings described by Rahner and therefore spiritual in the sense claimed by the classical European tradition.

These features attach to that general dependence of persons on relationships with other persons for the exercise, development and fulfilment of the capacities that define them as persons. The freedom, for instance, that characterises persons as self-conscious and self-determining beings, is found to develop in direct and not inverse proportion to the degree of strictly personal dependence of persons on other persons. Put more simply: the more I am subject to a *certain kind* of influence of other persons, the more (and not the less) self-determining I become. Such a paradoxical freedom-in-dependence is inexplicable both in terms of a scientific notion of causality and in terms of a materialist metaphysics. It is nevertheless corroborated by a phenomenology that has learnt from Thomist metaphysics, as I presently hope to show.

The work of Thomist phenomenologists, together with that of Rahner, thus provides hope of uniting the relational with the spiritual view of persons. Rahner himself does not attempt this in any systematic way; the work of those other writers who follow him to which I have referred, shows that it can be done. The account that I shall give is really an elaboration and systematisation of what they have done. If our hope is well founded we shall not only have found a way of overcoming both dualism and materialism, but also have constructed a solid philosophical framework in which the distinctive African insights into human nature contained in *umuntu ngumuntu ngabantu* and *seriti* will be at home.

In what follows I propose firstly to give a slightly more detailed account of what it is for persons to be self-realising (my term) in the sense understood by modern Thomists. This account is based on an analysis of certain rational acts of individual persons, in particular the making of judgments as to the truth of beliefs and of decisions based on insights into the goodness of actions. I then consider the necessary conditions that need to be met if persons are actually to exercise and develop their capacity for self-realisation. These conditions turn out to be the understanding and affirming presence of other persons in whom this capacity is already fully developed. Finally the conclusion that persons depend on other persons for the exercise and development of their capacity for self-realisation is examined in view of the apparent contradiction it contains, namely that personal freedom depends on the influence of others, and certain further consequences of this conclusion are brought to light. We will then be in a position to relate our philosophical theory of persons both to the conception contained in traditional African thought and to the intellectual situation of contemporary Africa.

Chapter Seven

A Philosophy for Africa

In this chapter I propose to give a summary account of a philosophy of human persons that draws its inspiration from the Thomist philosophical tradition as described in the previous chapter, and which is also able to give systematic expression to the African insights we described in Chapter Five. The summary is my own, though drawing on the work of many others in this tradition and outside it. It is impossible for me to present their contributions in detail here; I will however refer the reader to their work at the appropriate stage as I proceed.

Persons are self-realising

As we have already seen, to say that human beings have a capacity for self-realisation is one way of picking out what it is that makes them persons or rational, and so spiritual, beings. In ordinary speech what I call self-realisation is called freedom, that freedom which both as a fact and a value is inseparable from human life. But freedom is such an ambiguous word that I prefer to use the technical term for the sake of clarity.

The two most common signs of freedom or self-realisation in our everyday lives are our capacity to know the truth and our sense of responsibility. In everyday life we take both for granted. We would be stupid not to. Total skepticism about our ability to know the truth about things is a self-refuting attitude, as Aristotle showed when he got the skeptic to speak: even the skeptic meant his claim "There's no such thing as truth" to be taken as true. And there is something similarly indubitable about our sense of being ultimately responsible for certain of our actions, namely those we have deliberately decided on. However much we believed in determinism of some kind or another we would still retain this sense of responsibility for those acts we had deliberately decided on.

What both these unavoidable and undeniable experiences show is that persons have a capacity for what I will call self-realisation. In judgments of truth and deliberate decisions I am self-realising both in the sense that it is me and not another who is responsible for the act, and also that, whatever the object of the act may be, in performing it I also act upon myself. I am both free from the determining influence of external causes, and able to determine the sort of person I shall become.

These are such philosophically significant claims to make about persons that we must consider the evidence for our being self-realising more closely.

In making a judgment about the world (say "That is a cat") we certainly do claim to have grasped reality, even if sometimes we have to qualify what we say with a "probably". Even if we always had to say (which we don't) "It only seems so to me," we would still be claiming that it really did seem so to me, and not that it only seemed to seem so. One cannot get away from the scandalous claim to truth. And in claiming truth for one's judgment one is simultaneously affirming the distinction and the correspondence between one's ideas and the world. Truth is the correspondence between our ideas and the world, and for there to be a correspondence there must be a distinction. And because there is distinction there can also be error: one's ideas could fail to correspond to reality. Thus in making a judgment one reflects on one's own ideas about what one has experienced and compares them with the experience. The discovery of a point of correspondence constitutes evidence for the truth of the idea and we judge it to be true for that reason. For example: I am afraid of dogs. I am not sure whether the black dog in the house at the end of the road is dangerous or not. Then I see it muzzled when out on a walk, and so I judge that it is.

There are two things I want to draw attention to in this account of making a judgment. The first is that judgment always involves a reason, even if it is not explicitly adverted to. If I was asked afterwards "Why do you think that?" I could give a reason, even if only an obviously bad one. It would always make sense for someone to ask me "Why?" The second point is that in making a judgment I become present to myself and act on my self in a peculiar and radical way. It is my own idea that I am judging, and my own experience that provides the evidence for my judgment. The content of the idea and the judgment is the same: all that is added is the affirmation. In making a judgment of truth I assess my own beliefs by means of a criterion that I impose. In doing so I take up a point of view that is beyond my whole system of beliefs, in order to survey them and determine the coherence of the belief I am assessing with the system as a whole. This capacity to objectify and critically assess one's own beliefs is sometimes called the ability to abstract. It is an example of our ability to act upon oneself and be present to oneself as a whole.

From this it can be seen that our capacity for self-realisation and our capacity for logic (our demand for reasons for belief) are closely connected in the making of a judgment. The same is true in the making of a deliberate decision.

Here it is our desires that we have to consider rather than our beliefs. In making a decision we have to choose between a variety of different and often competing desires. This choice of what desire to act upon is consent. By consenting to this or that desire I allow it to determine how I shall act. Of course my desires and my consent only exist in a context of beliefs. I consent to a desire for some or other reason, because I believe such and such to be the case, that such and such a state of affairs will make me happy. Consent is not the same as having a reason but it takes place for a reason – at least when my decision is deliberate.

Once again it can be seen that in consenting to this or that desire I happen to have, I act upon myself. I have the capacity to create an internal division within myself and let the one side act upon the other. This is an inaccurate way of putting it since it is not a part of me that acts on another part, but simply me that acts on myself. I as consenting act upon myself as desiring: the actual content or object of the desire and the consent is the same. A consented-to desire is simply more my own, more me, than one I have not consented to. Here the way in which, by consenting to my desires, I bring myself to act is especially clear. I am self-realising in a very complete and comprehensive sense. And at the heart of my self-realisation is my capacity for logic, my acting for a reason.

It is because judgments and decisions are both things that we do for a reason that they cannot be the result of external causes acting upon us, but are instead signs of our capacity for self-realisation. The reason why no cause of the kind the sciences can discover could cause my grasp of the logical link between beliefs and desires whereby one of them could serve as the reason for the other being true, or the reason why I should decide on one act rather than another, is because that act of grasping can only properly be described in logical terms and not in physical or psychological ones. Psychological and physical explanations of my judgments and decisions will of necessity always leave out that I am doing what I do for a reason, that is because I have grasped a logical connection between one belief and another, or between a belief and a desire. Because physical and psychological events cannot be properly described in logical terms, they cannot be sufficient causes of events that can only be properly so described.

Let me clarify the rather abstract argument above with an example. I and a neighbour both believe that the black dog in the corner house is dangerous. I, as I have said, believe this because I have noticed that it is muzzled when taken walking. My neighbour, on the other hand, has not noticed this. He believes it is dangerous because he was bitten by a black dog in childhood and ever since has been afraid of black dogs.

Let us suppose that we are equally committed to our beliefs; they are equally strongly held and therefore equally able to determine our conduct. I however believe what I do for a reason. I believe that dogs wear muzzles to stop them biting and the black dog wears a muzzle. My belief about muzzles provides a logical link with my belief about the black dog. I believe what I do because of my grasp of this logical link. My belief has been caused by my grasp. For that reason in holding it I am self-realising, in acting upon it I act freely. In the case of my neighbour however this is not so. His belief is merely the result of the association of ideas; it could equally well have been caused by a drug or a bit of bone pressing on the brain. It is not caused by his grasp of any logical link between the blackness of the dog and its dangerousness. We would be right in recognising his belief, and the behaviour based on it, as compulsive, unfree.

I hope that I have been able to give some positive content to the idea that persons are self-realising. I also hope that it has become clear that insofar as we are self-realising we transcend the influence of any conceivable system of the kind of causes that the sciences can discover. By saying that we are free in this sense I do not of course mean that in human beings the laws of physics and biology cease to hold. Nor are we free from the law of gravity or the second law of thermodynamics. I do want to claim however that our behaviour cannot be *fully* accounted for by scientific laws of whatever kind. Nor is it produced by the chance or random action of material causes. It can only be explained in the last resort as the product of an entirely unique kind of causal agent, one that works according to logical laws and which we normally call a person. So metaphysical materialism cannot be true. Persons are however causes of things happening in the material world studied by the sciences: we are in continuous causal interaction with our material environment. So it is difficult to see how dualism could be true either.

Persons are other-dependent

I will now proceed to give a summary but systematic account of the necessary conditions for persons to exercise, develop and fulfill the natural capacities that define them as persons, namely the capacities that enable us to be self-realising in the sense I have just described.

In what follows I will use the work of (but not continually refer to) the phenomenological philosophers I have already referred to, both the Thomist ones and others. Thus the material I use is not original, though the form I give it, and in particular the way it is systematised, together with one or two conclusions I draw from it, are my own.

It must be remembered that the descriptions of the interpersonal transactions that form the necessary conditions for personal life and growth are intended to be philosophical. In other words they are derived from reflection on and analysis of our own fundamental and unavoidable experience of being a person, namely of self-realisation. They are thus ideal and abstract rather than realistic and concrete. They are not intended to be scientific, though I will refer to relevant scientific work in passing. With this having been said let me now proceed to set them out.

We have already seen that the idea that persons need other persons in order to realise their personhood is an important, though fairly recent, one in European thought, both philosophical and scientific.

How deeply we depend on our relationships with other persons to be persons is well illustrated by the case of "wild children", that is children who have been left to die at birth but for one reason or another have not died, but have grown to physical maturity (often in the company of animals) totally outside the society of other persons. In the few cases that there are on record, one thing is quite clear. The capacities that define us as persons (our ability to make reasoned judgments and responsible decisions, even our ability to think in concepts, and probably even real self-awareness) simply had not developed at all in these children. They looked like human beings but it was impossible to treat them properly as persons.

For a philosophical discussion of this phenomenon and the light it throws on the interpersonal conditions determining the acquisition of language and the ability to think conceptually, I would refer the reader to Suzanne Langer's *Philosophy in a New Key* (1971).

Recent experiments done by Rene Spitz and others into "hospitalism" in babies, confirm this conclusion (Ver Eecke, 1975). Babies, separated for one reason or another from their parents and cared for in institutions, developed as persons at a rate drastically slower than normal babies. The cause of this had nothing to do with the individual babies. Spitz' experiments established quite clearly that it was the lack of personal contact that inhibited their personal development. The institutions were overcrowded; the nurses had no time to do more than attend to the physical needs of the children. In particular there was never time for them to relate to the babies *as persons*, expressing recognition and love. The result of this lack of genuine personal contact, in every case, was a complete failure to develop the self-awareness and self-control of normal babies, a lack of development that showed itself in all sorts of terrible psychological syndromes and in physical problems as well.

It is in fact hardly necessary to stress how much our thoughts and behaviour are influenced by others and by our whole social milieu. It has become a commonplace of contemporary science. But what people are often not conscious of is the radically materialistic and deterministic conception of humanity that underlies the theories, the methods and the results of the human sciences. Materialism and determinism are in fact built into the very notion of science itself. It would be unscientific to allow for an inner life of persons, a life that escapes objective observation. It would also be unscientific to consider inter-personal influences that can't be measured or fitted into law-like generalizations in any way.

Thus the idea that persons depend on an environment of other persons for their personal development, as it has developed in the modern period, is inseparable from the generally materialistic world-view of science, a world-view in which human beings are simply one species of complex biological organism among others, and whose behaviour being subject to the same natural laws can be understood in the same way as any other species. I want to include the undeniable truth that persons do depend on persons and their whole social environment for their development, in my conception of humanity. But I want to exclude the materialism and the determinism.

On the face of it it may seem that the two elements of my conception of humanity are simply incompatible. How *can* one be both self-enacting, free, and dependent on other persons in so radical a way for one's development as a person. The very notion of a person as a free being and that of being dependent for one's personhood on others seems to be contradictory. In the rest of this chapter I want to try and show that they are not. And even more, I want to show that it is only through a certain kind of dependence on other persons that personal freedom actually comes into being, grows and is perfected.

I find it useful to consider the dependence of persons on other persons for their personal development in three. stages. At each stage the fundamental pattern is the same, but each stage of personal development supplies us with its own special features and so helps to build up a more sensitive and comprehensive understanding of what is actually taking place.

The three stages of personal growth

The first stage is the development of the bare capacity for self-realisation to the normal (adult) point where one is able to make reasoned judgments and deliberate decisions. At this stage our self-realisation takes the form of self-consciousness and self-determination, or better, consciousness of one-self as self-determining, an origin of free action in the world

The second stage is that of moral or spiritual or psychological growth. Here growth in self-enactment takes the form of growth in self-knowledge and self-affirmation. As we shall see it is also a growth in integration of the person, of their cognitive, volitional and emotional life.

The third stage is not really a stage at all, but the state towards which personal development tends and the activity in which it finds its full expression. Here self-realisation takes the form of self-transcendence and self-donation. Let us now consider these three stages each in turn. This way of approach is inspired by that of John Macmurray, and especially by his Gifford Lectures of 1953 – 1954, published as *The Self as Agent* and *Persons in Relation* (1957;1959). In spite of the merit of this pioneering work it lacks something in philosophical rigour. It makes up for this, though, by its suggestiveness and provocativeness.

The first stage

To grasp our need for other persons in the first stage of our personal development, it will be helpful to visualize the relationship between a baby and its parent (let us say, a mother). The baby stands for the bare natural capacity for personal growth, the mother for whatever is necessary for this capacity to develop, the child's whole personal milieu.

It is important to note that there *is* a natural capacity. Humans have it at birth, and chimpanzees don't. A famous case illustrating this is that of the Kellogs, an American scientific couple who brought up their own child and a baby chimp born at the same time in an absolutely identical way. At first it was the chimp who far outstripped the child in its development, rapidly acquiring all sorts of practical skills and exhibiting a highly developed practical intelligence. Eventually however the child began to develop the symbolic use of language as a form of self-expression and from then on the difference in kind between the capacities of chimp and child became rapidly apparent (Kellog and Kellog, 1933).

One has only to ask the question as to what is required for a natural capacity of this kind to develop to realize that at least the presence of another person is needed. For without the presence of another person there is nothing in the world that can reflect the child back to itself as precisely a "being with a self". The child is certainly not self-conscious from the start; on the contrary its consciousness is initially extroverted. And no natural object, even an animal, is capable of responding to it precisely as a (potentially) self-conscious being. What is required, at the very least, is the presence of another person who is conscious of the child as a person and who actually directs their consciousness towards the child. In more concrete terms, what is required is someone who both recognizes and treats the child as a person. It is only in the directed gaze of the mother that the child can discover itself as the object of the mother's attention. And it is only in the mother's acceptance of its responsive activities that it can get a sense of itself as a subject, as a real origin of action in the world.

One can gain further insight into the nature of this fundamental interpersonal transaction in which, far beyond the reaches of memory, our *own* personal development began, if one will perform the following experiment. Take a partner and look into her eyes. Look at the eyes themselves one by one as an eye-doctor might. Then turn your attention to her gaze. Notice the difference. In one and the same moment you pick up her presence as a person and the fact that she is looking at you. You still see her eyes but they are not *what* you see. You see a person. And at the same time you become conscious of yourself as the one who is looked at.

Her eyes are necessary for you to grasp her presence in her gaze, but experiments have shown that when you are picking up her gaze you are not in fact looking *at* her eyes. Your visual attention oscillates rapidly from eye to eye or else is fixated on some indeterminate point between them. The presence of one person to another is not simply a physical event or process. (An excellent account of this intersubjective discovery of self is provided by John Heron in his phenomenological study of mutual gazing (1970:243–264).

Though the presence of another person is necessary it is not sufficient for the child to develop a consciousness of itself as self-determining. A nurse in an orphanage who cared simply for its physical needs and who did so without any sense of vocation but simply as a way of earning her living would not be sufficient. Why? Because she would not be present, or present fully, *as a person*. Her hands and eyes would be present as the meeters of needs. But she wouldn't put *herself* into her actions. She would not give her consent, her heart, her love, to the baby, and for this reason she would not make herself fully present to the baby as the person who she is. And in thus withholding herself she would fail to treat it and affirm it as a person itself. Without being able to discover itself as a person in the relationship with the nurse the baby would not be able to develop a properly personal self-consciousness at all.

On the other hand if the baby is recognized and valued for its own sake by a loving mother there is no impediment in her whole-hearted affirmative presence to it and thus no impediment to its discovery of itself in its relationship with her. Further, it is only in the case of a loving mother, that the child's happy response to her expressions of love will be what she most desires for herself and so make her happy too.

Thus it is only in such a case that the baby can be the source of real power (power to make the mother happy). And thus it is only in this case that the conditions exist for it to become conscious of itself as a real (powerful) origin of action and of changes in the world. In other words it is only in this way that it can begin to become conscious of itself as a self-determining being, a consciousness that is progressively reinforced in the daily dialogue between it and the inviting, responsive mother.

Our conclusion to the first stage is thus that persons depend on the caring, attentive, consenting presence of other persons if they are to develop their capacity for self-realisation to the point of becoming conscious of themselves as self-determining agents in the world.

For a more detailed account of this stage, with references to other writers, I would refer the reader to my article, "What makes us persons?" (1984:67–79).

The second stage

The second stage in the development of persons is the development of self-knowledge and self-affirmation. These are the forms taken by self-real-isation at this stage, self-knowledge being a development of the simple consciousness of oneself as an agent into an ever deeper insight into the unique person that one is, and self-affirmation a development of one's capacity for self-determination so that one becomes progressively more able to fully accept and express the person one is becoming.

To show the need that we have of other persons in order to grow in self-knowledge and self-affirmation it is necessary to say a little more about the self, the properly personal self, whose development we are trying to understand.

Persons are self-realising. This means, as we saw earlier, that within the unity of our personal being there is the duality of being both subject and object of all our acts. We are aware of and act upon ourselves. And this duality is what makes us persons. Moreover the duality in ourselves is not something fixed or static. It is actually a duality of active relationships or movements, and these active relationships constitute the personal self. The first is the movement of division through which the self becomes aware of itself and knows itself. The second is a movement of unification through which the self accepts and affirms itself as known and so comes to possess itself, to be itself, more fully.

A good illustration of these elements in the self can be seen with reference to psychoanalysis. In the process of psycho-analysis one comes slowly to a deeper insight into the person that one is. One discovers why one behaves compulsively in certain situations. At first however one resists the insight; one finds it hard to accept oneself as that sort of person. Gradually however with the help of the analyst one overcomes one's fear and comes to accept the new insight into oneself. And as one does so one becomes progressively freed of one's compulsion. One is now in full possession of that part of oneself that previously was beyond one's control. One has in fact become "more oneself".

What previously had enjoyed only a "shadowy" existence on the periphery of the self, is now drawn into the centre and in the process becomes more real, more really me. This is the typical character of the process of self-realisation.

I have said that these two relationships that the self has to itself, the relationships of self-knowledge and of self-affirmation, actually constitute the self. By that I mean that they are not external to but internal to the self; they make the personal self the sort of thing it is. There is however a third element in the self that I haven't mentioned but whose reality is implied by the reality of the other two. This is the self as origin and end of self-knowledge and self-affirmation, the point from which the inner movement of personal life begins and to which it returns. This element of the self as the origin of the inner movement of the self can be understood as desire, the fundamental desire to be, to be a person, to be myself, that wells up from the centre of my being and shows itself in the never-ending quest for happiness and fulfilment.

So there are three elements in or aspects of the self, one characterized by knowledge, one by affirmation and one by desire. I shall call them the cognitive, the volitional and the emotional systems of the self. I call them systems because of course each of them contains many different items. We know lots of details about oneself; our lives are full of different choices; our desires are as many and varied as the plants of the earth. On the other hand, in spite of the sheer number and variety of our beliefs, our choices and our desires, there is in each sphere of our lives, a pressure towards unity and coherence, consistency and order. For these two reasons I call these elements of the self systems.

With this idea of the self in mind we can understand better what self-knowledge and self-affirmation are. To get to know myself I need to discover what I believe, what I value and what I desire. More especially I need to discover my *habitual* beliefs, commitments and desires, since these habits of belief, choice and desire are closer to the centre of myself, most truly *me*. Ultimately what is most fundamental and central to the self are my desires. So real self-knowledge must be based on an insight into what I really desire, which of my desires are the most central to and important in my life. True self-affirmation, on the other hand, will consist in a whole-hearted consent to these desires and the attempt to realize them in my life.

For this way of treating the topic of the knowledge of persons I am indebted to the little-known work of Cirne-Lima (1965).

The idea that self-knowledge and self-affirmation, and hence personal growth, consist essentially in discovering and satisfying my most fundamental and all-pervading desires may seem strange at first. It will I think seem less so when we consider what these desires are. They are not just any desires . To see this, consider this quotation from D. H. Lawrence:

"All that matters is that men and women should do what they really want to do. Though here as elsewhere" (he is discussing our sexual life) "we must remember that man has a double set of desires, the shallow and the profound, the personal, superficial, temporary desires and the inner, impersonal, great desires that are fulfilled in long periods of time. The desires of the moment are easy to recognize, but the others, the deeper ones, are difficult. It is the business of our Chief Thinkers to tell us of our deeper desires, not to keep shrilling our little desires into our ears" (1931:52–53).

It is these "deep desires" that we must come to know and affirm if we are to develop as persons. That being said, it is important to realize the genuinely "deep" desires are not desires that we just happen to have acquired in the course of our upbringing and education, or desires that are caused in us by a particular cultural context. (Say, the desire to watch videos!) The deep desires are those that are common to everyone because they emanate from human nature itself. They may express and even satisfy themselves differently in different societies and at different periods of history but at heart they are the same in everyone: the desire to love and be loved, the desire to understand, the desire to create, the desire to play, to laugh, to worship ... the list is endless.

But self-knowledge is not just a matter of learning a list. Nor is it even a question of gaining an understanding of human nature in the way I am attempting here. One has to gain a knowledge of these desires and come to affirm them *in oneself*. One has actually to feel, to taste them as they manifest themselves in one's own life, and to be able to distinguish the deep from the superficial.

An example may make this clearer. In the sphere of our sexuality, for instance, we may be aware of a number of desires. We may have a desire for frequent casual sexual intercourse with a variety of partners, as well as a desire for an enduring, whole-hearted sexual communion with one other person. Self-knowledge here would consist in being aware of both desires but in recognizing the superficiality of the one and the centrality and importance of the other. One would have to become aware of the compulsive and dissipating character of the superficial desire as well as the enduring and unifying character of the deep desire. And such an awareness would issue in a judgment of value concerning the role to be played by the different desires in one's life, of the degree to which one ought to consent to them in the decisions that one makes.

Now that we have a better idea of what it is to know and affirm oneself we can go on to see how we depend on other persons in order to get to know and affirm ourselves properly. Before we do so, though, let me remind you that we are considering the second stage of our development as persons, which is to say self-realising (free) beings. In what way is a growth in self-knowledge and self-affirmation a growth in freedom?

I think one can begin to see an answer to this question if one envisages the actual process of personal development in a more concrete way. Initially, or in the early stages of the process, the actual life of persons is characterized by all sorts of conflict. There is conflict within each system of the self – between contradictory beliefs, incompatible choices and warring desires. There is also conflict between the systems – between what I believe I ought to do and what I do, between what I choose to do and what I want to do, between what I want and what I judge to be right. This is, more or less, the state of soul of everyone in process of development.

It is not difficult to see that in such a state of inner division my behaviour is bound to be more or less compulsive, and hence unfree. If my self-knowledge is incomplete then I do not know what I really want. I will not know which desires to consent to and which to inhibit. Insofar as I encourage the superficial desires I will increase the division in myself since the deep desires which I am suppressing will not go away but instead persist in growing opposition to the rest.

In such a state of division it will be impossible to affirm myself whole-heartedly. I may strive to do so, but the self that I am affirming in such a state is not my true self, and affirming it merely makes matters worse. Attempts to affirm a mistaken image of myself against my deep desires builds up habits of thought and action that militate against real self-knowledge. In order to maintain the illusory harmony and identity I have constructed I suppress all awareness of my real desires and all recognition of beliefs that contradict my illusions. So it is a vicious circle: lack of self-knowledge makes genuine self-affirmation impossible, the inability to affirm oneself whole-heartedly prevents real self-knowledge. This is the nature of the tendency of the conflict in the self; it is a tendency to disintegration.

Against this background it should not be too difficult to see self-knowledge and self-affirmation as principles of integration in the self and hence the cause of a progressive increase of personal freedom.

True self-knowledge is not only an awareness of our desires, it is also an insight into their relative centrality and importance. It is able to distinguish the deep from the superficial and rank them accordingly. Insofar as we consent to this ranking and allow this order to appear in our choices and our acts, appropriate habits of desire will be built up and the conflict between the systems of the self will be progressively overcome. Our beliefs, our commitments and, essentially, our desires themselves will conform to the same true pattern. The pattern discovered by self-knowledge will be whole-heartedly affirmed and come to be reflected in our actual emotional life. And because the pattern is genuine, the source of conflict within each system will have been removed as well. Our beliefs about what is really valuable will not conflict with each other. Nor will our commitments. And nor, eventually, will our desires themselves.

Self-knowledge is the principle of integration within each system, the cognitive, the volitional and the emotional, while self-affirmation is the principle of integration between them. Together they are the cause of a progressive increase in freedom.

For a profound study of the role of the will in personal growth, and in particular its unifying function in the person, I would refer the reader to Austin Farrer's (unfortunately very difficult) *Finite and Infinite* (1979).

Of course in real life conflict is never completely overcome. Nor are self-knowledge and self-affirmation ever complete. But that need not affect the approximate accuracy of the account of personal growth just given. Let us assume that it is more or less true, and now try to see in what way its occurrence in us depends on other persons.

The interpersonal transaction I summarise here is dealt with in greater detail in the second volume of Macmurray's Gifford Lectures referred to above, *Persons in Relation* (1959), in M. Nédoncelle's *Love and the Person* (1966), and in a strange but perceptive article by L. Feldstein, 'Personal Freedom: The Dialectics of Self-Possession'(1976:61–85).

We have already seen that, lacking self-knowledge and self-affirmation, I am unable to acquire them on my own. What I need is to get to know and affirm someone who both knows and affirms themselves. The relationship I am describing is that of (a perfect) friendship, and not necessarily a sexual one. To keep this before the reader's mind I will assume, since I am a man and heterosexual, that the friend described here also is.

In getting to know my friend I am getting to know the deep desires of our common nature as they manifest themselves in him. And insofar as I really come to know him as he knows himself, I come to share his own judgment of their relative importance. Moreover acquaintance with them in him puts me in touch with them in myself. To the degree that I come to affirm my friend, to value and love him, I affirm the pattern of desires that constitutes his character and identity. And so I am able to affirm them in myself as well.

So far, so good. But how can I get to know my friend in such a deep way and affirm him so whole-heartedly when I am as yet incapable of knowing or affirming even myself properly?

The answer is, my friend enables me to. He does this by first knowing and affirming me. He knows me, after all, better than I know myself. He is aware of the deep desires that underlie my incoherent and compulsive behaviour. He knows what will really make me happy. And he is able to affirm me in a way I cannot affirm myself. He affirms my deep desires in spite of the fact that they are hidden. Such affirmation may well include criticism of my behaviour, since that is the product of a misguided consent to superficial desires. But fundamentally it will consist in a real and really disinterested desire for my good, for my growth as a person. And since, deep down, this is really what I want too, his affirmation of me will make for my consent. His affirmation of me will enable me to "open up" to him. Insofar as I open up to him I will begin to affirm him. This will enable me to get to know him better and so to affirm him more. In this way the transaction between us will be set in motion resulting eventually in my growing in self-knowledge and self-affirmation through my growth in knowledge and affirmation of him.

It is now evident why we need other persons to grow in self-knowledge and self-affirmation. And why they must be persons who both know and affirm themselves. This is then our conclusion to the second stage of personal growth: persons depend on other persons who have already developed as persons if they are to develop their capacity for self-realisation to the full.

The second stage of personal growth is dealt with in greater detail, with references to the body of literature it represents, in my 'A New Argument for the Existence of God' (1987:157–177).

The third stage

The third stage of personal development is that in which self-realisation takes the form of self-transcendence and self-donation. As I have said this third stage is concerned with the goal of all our personal growth and the activity that most properly expresses the fulfilment of personal growth. Of course our personal growth is never complete so this stage is not really a stage. But then of course neither are the first two either, in the sense of a strict temporal sequence. In the third stage we are really concerned with the kind of activity that properly expresses personal growth at whatever stage of personal development one has reached. Clearly if there is a typical form of activity expressive of personal growth, then the more one has developed as a person the more one will be able to engage in it. In this sense a description of it will be a description of the goal or state to which all personal growth tends.

At this stage then our job will be to show that persons stand in need of other persons in order properly to express the personal growth they have achieved however complete such growth might be.

At first sight the opposite might seem to be the case. To the extent that one has developed full self-knowledge and is fully self-affirming one would seem to need other persons less and not more. That may be true as far as the development of the capacities is concerned; it is not true when we consider how they are to be expressed.

What after all is the point of personal growth? It is the expression of a natural capacity in us and answers a natural desire. But capacities realize themselves in activities. What is the activity for the sake of which we desire to develop as persons? Is it perhaps simply self-knowledge and self-affirmation for their own sake? Surely not. Most people are not even aware that they want such things at all. There is a far more obvious, more convincing answer.

Each stage of our personal development has shown that our deepest, most central, need has been for other persons. The same is true here. But here we need other persons not in order to develop as persons, but simply *for their own sake*. In fact at this stage it is paradoxical to talk of *need*. It is simply what we want. We want the life-giving relationship with others to remain but now we want it not primarily for our sake but for theirs. To spell it out fully: we want to know and affirm them not primarily so that we will continue to develop as persons, but simply as an end in itself, because they are knowable and affirmable, because it is worthwhile.

In more concrete terms it amounts to this: we want to know fully and love genuinely those who know and love us. That is the ultimate goal of all personal growth, what I have called the third stage. And we want to be worth knowing fully and being loved by those who are worth knowing fully and being genuinely loved; that is the personal growth I have described in the first two stages. That is a secondary goal because a necessary means to the primary one. To put it all together, one can say that the ultimate goal of personal growth is the creation of a community of persons in full knowledge and genuine love of each other, a community in which I am enabled to participate through my own self-knowledge and self-affirmation.

There are so many good philosophical books on the topic of love that it seems invidious to single out some for special mention. I would mention here only those authors who are mainly Thomist in inspiration, and whose treatment of the topic is of a piece with mine. These are: G. Gilleman (1959), R. Johann (1966), M. Nédoncelle (1966), and J. Toner (1968).

There are some features of this stage of personal development that deserve special comment. The first is its *other*-centredness. It is the *other* person I am now concerned to know and love. And this in so complete and radical a manner as to entail what I have called self-transcendence and self-donation.

In the intimate knowledge of the other person that personal growth makes possible I enter so fully into his life and mind that it is as though I have overcome the limitations of my separate individuality. We seem to share a common mind. This is self-transcendence; you remain yourself but you have overcome your separateness and closedness so that you are able to fully enter into the life of another. The same is true of the love I have for the other person. It is he whom I love, and for his own sake, not just for mine. It is gift-love not need-love. And the gift is myself. This is self-donation. It is the attitude revealed in all genuine self-sacrifice, and also in that mysterious activity of human re-creation we call forgiveness. These are the usual forms it takes in a world containing suffering and moral evil. But we also get glimpses of its true glory in moments of ecstatic love, creative effort and the experience of beauty.

In addition to the distinctive other-centredness of the attitude and activity of a person in the third stage, there is a corresponding quality in the community of persons created by personal growth. It is characterized by a peculiar reciprocity and mutuality, even a unanimity, of mind and heart and feeling. But here, as in the other two stages, there is no question of a diminishment of personal freedom due to an absorption by other persons. The exact opposite is the case. Self-transcendence and self-donation represent the fullest expression of my freedom. In this kind of personal community my freedom is at last complete.

Finally, lest our whole account of personal growth (and especially our account of its fulfilment in the third stage), be dismissed as unrealistic and idealistic, let me add this qualification. There is a duality to human persons: they are self-realising but other-dependent. Put metaphorically: there is a centre and a periphery to the human self, a nucleus that is forming, and particles in orbit. There is the full self-consciousness and self-determination of our deepest beliefs and most unconditional commitments, and there is the near-unconsciousness and near-inertness of our fingernails and our hair – and every degree of self-consciousness and self-determination in between. There is no discontinuity between inner and outer, between centre and periphery, as the dualists maintain.

What I have been describing in my account of the three stages of personal development is really the growth of the centre, the nucleus, of a person. And of course in the real circumstances of human life there can be radical discontinuity between the inner self and its outer expression. Any particular outward act may not properly express the stage to which the inner self has grown. Even habits of action can contradict the character of the inner self; an alcoholic can be a wise and loving person. The development and the dynamisms that I have described are to a large extent hidden, undercover, even unconscious, ones, often obscured or distorted by the immediate happenings of life. There can be no doubt however that they are real, that it is really they, and not the more obvious and dramatic actions and reactions in social life, that give our lives their true character and direction.

Chapter Eight

Beyond Materialism and Dualism

We have now come to the end of my description of the necessary conditions for human persons to exercise, develop and fulfill those capacities that define us as persons. It appears that we have a peculiar need of certain kinds of relationship with other persons if we are to develop our capacity for self-realisation.

I hope that the relevance of my account of the necessary conditions for us to grow as persons, for our understanding and evaluation of the African idea of *umuntu ngumuntu ngabantu,* is clear. I have tried to show how our dependence on our social milieu of other persons for our own development need not be destructive of that freedom of choice and action that is the essence of being a person.

There is always a danger that the African idea of community can be understood in such a way that individual freedom and responsibility is undermined, especially in the context of authoritarian political attitudes or superstitious beliefs relating to physical and psychic health, as pointed out by Wiredu and others. My account reveals that even the most radical and all-pervasive influence of other persons on me need not diminish my freedom of choice and action as long as this influence is a strictly personal one; it must be the effect of an attitude that is expressive of the genuine personal growth and fulfilment of the other person. Such an attitude of wise and loving affirmation of me, emanating from the other's clear-sighted and whole-hearted acceptance of themselves, actually enhances and promotes my freedom through a progressive integration of my cognitive, volitional and emotional life.

A moral idea

As long as this condition is met, the more fully I am involved in community with others the more completely I am able to realise my own deep desires to the full. The good of the community (in which I am also involved) will be my highest value, just as traditional African thought would expect. At the same time, the influence of the community on me is what enables me to achieve this form of self-transcendence and self-donation which is the fullest expression of my own self-realisation. The aim of ethical and political life and thought is to discover, in the particular economic and geographical circumstances in which we live, the practices and institutions that best embody this ideal. It may, for instance, be the case, even in an industrialised urban environment, that some form of clan or kinship system is the best support for family life. It may also be the case in a wage and cash economy that such a practice as *lobola* (a form of "bride-price" in which a number of cattle or their cash equivalent is given to the family of the bride) is not compatible with the kind of interpersonal transactions outlined above.

The account I have given of the necessary conditions for personal growth has clear ethical implications. The notion of growth itself is a normative one. In a genuinely philosophical context it can't be understood in a merely scientific-psychological way – as the achievement of genital primacy for instance, or of a maturity that is defined in terms of adjustment to a particular (and merely contingent) social situation. The ethical standards are not relative to this or that culture but derive from our nature as persons. Admittedly, as in the above account, these transcendent moral standards are very general. But that is as it should be. They are not vacuous. They have the same kind of generality as the fundamental human needs identified by classical Thomist natural law theory, or of the basic characteristics of the *umuntu*, the fully-grown person of traditional African wisdom. Certain kinds of individual attitude and social practice are clearly identified as incompatible with human flourishing. Acquisitive and competitive individualism (as embodied in European capitalism and permitted by liberal political theory) as well as totalitarianism (as fostered by all forms of socialism) are equally alien to the spirit of the conception of humanity I have outlined. In considering the political predicament of contemporary Africa we shall have to give some thought to alternative social and economic arrangements that are more consonant with this conception.

What I have tried especially to bring out in the outline I have given, as far as the moral dimension of personal life is concerned, is the lack of opposition between the individual and the common good. Not only is the other-affirming attitude the key to my own integration and growth; it is what will in the last resort most satisfy and fulfill me. The sterile debate between egoism and altruism is seen to be misconceived. Egoism, as making my own satisfaction the condition for all my activity, is always wrong. Altruism, as seeking the good of the other for their own sake, is always right. What the above account shows is why this is so. Egoism is wrong because it is self-destructive; altruism right because it builds me up.

Here one must distinguish between the reason why the one is right and the other wrong from the motive with which I seek the one and avoid the other. I affirm the other for their own sake, not in order to build myself up. If I didn't, I wouldn't be built up in that way; our community and its effects on me wouldn't be genuine. At the same time as affirming the other for their own sake (in whatever way and in whatever circumstances I do this), I do in fact build myself up, and can clear-sightedly be aware of this. In fact as a morally wise good person I ought to want it. But this is not egoism. I do not want it so that I can pat myself on the back. I want to develop my powers to the full so that I can more fully know and affirm the other, be an altruist with all my mind and heart. This will certainly give me pleasure, and the most satisfying pleasure. But the pleasure is not the motive but the concomitant of the altruism. Were it the motive (that is, I think, logically conceivable, though very odd), it would vitiate the altruism and hence any pleasure that resulted would not be the kind of pleasure that is the concomitant of altruism only. In this way the above analysis shows the interdependence of the individual and the common good. This is something significant for moral thinking in general, but especially so for African thought where the tendency is to over-ride the individual for the collective's sake.

The distinctive feature of the account I have given of human community, which makes it different from most European conceptions but consonant with traditional African ones, derives from the way that human persons are understood in contemporary Thomist thought. The paradoxical dependence on others for one's own self-realisation in the course of one's personal growth is simply the concrete expression in the social world of the duality of relations that actually constitutes the human person, the relation-to-self that is our spirituality and the relation-to-other that is our materiality. And this duality is, as we saw, the expression in space and time of that duality inherent in the unity of a person as such, by virtue of which persons are both present to themselves and self-determining.

I have argued that such an understanding of human persons is incompatible both with a materialist and with a dualist view of the world. Now the fact that the Thomist view of persons offers an alternative to both dualism and materialism appears in the above account when we consider the nature of the influence of one person on another that is productive of personal growth. In this distinctively "interpersonal causality" we have the manifestation of a reality that cannot be accounted for by either a materialistic or a dualistic metaphysics. We are obliged to recognise a form of energy or power that is unlike anything scientifically demonstrable but is on the other hand similar in many ways to that which traditional African thought identifies by the name of *seriti*.

Interpersonal causality

That there is something peculiar in the influence of persons on other persons that leads to personal growth, is evident when it is remembered that personal growth is a growth in freedom and self-realisation. The greater the *strictly personal* influence you have on me, the freer I become. The more you are involved *in a strictly personal way* in the production of my act, the more the act is my own. The kind of causality here is different in kind from that recognised by any science. This is of course most clearly seen in the strictly physical realm where action and reaction are equal and opposite. In the common production of work by two distinct causes, the more that is done by one the less is done by the other.

Think of two oxen pulling a plough. The logic of scientific causality entails that a plurality of causes implies a common measure in terms of which the effect of each can be guaged and either added to or subtracted from that of the other. In the case of the interpersonal transactions I have described there is no common measure. The personal growth produced is wholly the work of the other; it is also wholly my own. So it is not, strictly speaking, produced by our co-operation; co-operation implies the addition of two distinct amounts of energy or power. And that is not what happens. My response to the other is wholly the work of the other; it is also wholly my own. This indicates the incommensurability of the strictly personal influences emanating from persons in the kind of inter-personal relations I have described.

A metaphysical consequence of this is that one is forced to recognise the reality of a form of energy, and so too of a source of energy, and thus a kind of being, that transcends the material realm which is the proper object of the sciences. One could call it spiritual energy if that did not imply dualism. Because recognition of its reality need not imply dualism. As we have seen the traditional African concept of *seriti* does not entail a dualistic world view.

This idea of a strictly personal dimension of reality that transcends anything explicable by the sciences, but which is recognised and richly described in traditional African thought, is corroborated by the work of the English phenomenologist John Heron. Basing his reflections on detailed empirical studies he is led to very similar philosophical conclusions to mine. For this reason I propose to quote him fairly extensively.

Heron's study focusses on the phenomenon of mutual gazing: me gazing at you gazing at me. In meeting your gaze it is not the physical properties of your eyes that I fix on, as, say, an eye-specialist would. The experimental work dealt with by Heron shows that in fact when I pick up your gaze my eyes actually either simply oscillate back and forth between your eyes, or else fixate on a point equidistant between them. What I pick up is the gaze, and in the gaze the presence of a person actively present to me. And the same is simultaneously true of you.

Heron concludes that careful attention to the phenomenon of mutual gazing forces us to recognise the reality of an interpersonal transaction that cannot either be reduced to a physical exchange nor (for a variety of reasons) be explained as some form of mental "projection". The physical interaction is of course necessary, but it is merely the vehicle for a strictly personal one that essentially transcends it. Heron is forced to coin the term "transphysical" to describe this sort of reality: "The luminosity of the gaze or the gaze-light of the other is a distinct phenomenal reality which is transphysical, although supervenient upon and mediated by physical phenomena: that is to say, it cannot be reduced to any purely physical luminosity of the eyes, to physical light reflected from the moistened and translucent surface of the cornea – although this may be a necessary physical condition for its optimal occurrence. In a sense, the gaze of the other just *is* this transphysical luminosity about his eyes, an extra phenomenal dimension refracted by their physical properties" (1970:253).

Nor is it only the object of my perception, the gaze of the other, that is transphysical; it is the activity of perception itself: "If the luminosity of the gaze of the other is a transphysical reality supervenient upon the physical properties of his eyes, then it follows that it is not perceived by me in terms of any purely physical – that is, retinal and cortical – processes: there is a transphysical as well as a physical activity involved in my perception of the gaze-light of the other" (1970:254).

Finally, by unpicking the full complexity of the intersubjective relationship of mutual gazing, Heron reaches the conclusion that there is a transphysical dimension to the whole interpersonal transaction, and so too to persons themselves: "Furthermore, there is a sense in which the inward streaming of the gaze of the other as received by me constitutes at that time the reality of my being: the gaze received openly and without fear can yield for me a profound awareness of my body-mind unity. In this situation the gaze of the other may illuminate me as a unitive being with no awareness of body-mind distinction. Similarly, I apprehend the other as a unitive presence revealed before me. But each of these unitive states is secondary to the unitive reality constituted by the relation of mutual gazing itself. The transphysical streaming of the gaze of the other interfuses my whole being, the transphysical streaming of my gaze interfuses the whole being of the other; but in each case this only occurs by virtue of the thorough interpenetration of the mutual streaming – which constitutes the dramatic elan of true encounter between persons. It is the interaction of the two-fold gazing which is a necessary condition of the irradiation of each by each being. This interpenetration, then, is a transphysical unitive reality or field – which is also a unitive field of consciousness – with two poles, the irradiated being of each. Within this unitive field, my awareness of myself is in part constituted by my awareness of his awareness of me, and my awareness of him is in part constituted by my awareness of his awareness of me; that is to say, my awareness of his awareness of me both reveals me to myself and reveals him to me, and his simultaneous awareness of my awareness of him both reveals him to himself and reveals me to him. But further, in my awareness of his awareness of my awareness, whether of myself or of him, I reveal myself to him; and in his awareness of my awareness of his awareness, whether of himself or me, he reveals himself to me. Thus in the unitive field of consciousness established through the interfused transphysical streaming of mutual gazing, each is revealed to himself, each is revealed to the other, and each reveals himself to the other. Because the gaze of each in part constitutes the being of the other only by virtue of the reciprocal interaction, there is a sense in which each is co-present at the opposite pole; that is to say, each has internal perception both of his own unitive being and of the unitive being of the other to some degree" (1970:255).

There are a couple of points worth emphasising in this long quotation. Firstly, in spite of the reality of the transphysical, dualism is time and again denied. This is the point of Heron's stress on the *unitive* character of what is observed, the activity of observing, and the reality underlying both. A second point to observe is how the relation of mutual gazing is simultaneously active and receptive, giving and receiving self-knowledge and knowledge of the other in the same act for each.

If Heron's descriptions are accurate then we have in them an impressive corroboration of the insights of traditional African thought into the nature of persons and personal interaction for which I have tried to provide a systematic philosophical framework. The empirical evidence on which they are based is undeniable, though of course one can try to interpret it in other ways. There are two arguments commonly brought against a thesis such as Heron's. The first is that what appears to be a property of the gaze itself is in fact an inference from a variety of observations of facial and bodily characteristics that is "projected" onto the gaze by the perceiver. The second is that our perception of the other's eyes causes in us an emotional reaction which we then project onto the eyes of the other.

However neither argument will work. Against the first is the established fact that the difference between the physical appearance of the eyes and the gaze-phenomenon itself is still perceptible even when the eyes are artificially isolated under experimental conditions from their normal facial surroundings. There is moreover a distinction between the emotional meanings borne by the gaze (which the argument asserts to be inferred from the non-ocular surroundings of the gaze), and the bare phenomenon of the gaze itself that reveals the presence of the other.

The second argument is also misconceived. An emotional response is a function of how one sees the world; it is caused by some cognitive apprehension of an object in the world, the eyes of the other in this case. If inference is ruled out, as we have shown it must be, then the emotion we find in the gaze is perceived by us directly and not "projected".

Heron's work thus supports my claim that it is because persons transcend materiality that the personal influence of one person on another is able to augment rather than diminish that person's freedom. The peculiar character of "interpersonal causality" that comes to light in my description of interpersonal relations is a consequence of the spirituality of persons.

In the above outline of my conception of human persons and community I have tried to give philosophical form to the intuitions embodied in the African ideas of *umuntu ngumuntu ngabantu* and *seriti*. I also hope that my account of these ideas has gone some way towards establishing their truth and importance. I have relied on contemporary Thomist philosophers and phenomenologists in this venture, but the final form and terminology is my own.

I now want to indicate how I think such a philosophy of persons can help us to understand the predicament we find ourselves in in South Africa today, and even suggest criteria for determining the goals, conduct and methods of the struggle for liberation in the various spheres of human life. First of all, however, I want to show how our philosophy of persons can provide us with a general insight into the nature of the lack or loss of freedom that constitutes the deepest level of the human predicament in whatever sphere of life.

Chapter Nine

The Human Predicament

I am concerned with the question as to whether philosophy can be of any help to us in the predicament in which we now find ourselves. Up to now I have spoken of Africa in a general way, of traditional African thought and contemporary African problems. In fact, however, it is my intention to focus on South Africa which is the only part of Africa I have personal experience of.

But are not South Africa's problems notoriously special to itself? At some levels this is true, but at the deepest level, where philosophy is truly at home, I think not. South Africa, after all, is part of Africa; the vast majority of its people have an African language as their home-language, and traditional African thought is part of their tradition.

South Africa is part of Africa, and Africa is part of the world. If Teilhard has taught us anything it is that we must try and see things in global terms. There is only one humanity, and human nature is the same in every part of the world.

It is for this reason that we can hope that philosophy can be of some help in our present struggle in South Africa. Philosophy offers us an insight into human nature that is deeper than any other; hence it if anything can enable us to see why it is that we should be in the predicament we are in. It can help us understand the predicament and give us the right terms with which to describe it. Above all it can give us an ethical understanding of it, of what aspects are bad and what aims are good.

It is easy enough to say, for instance, that Africa's problems are the problems of a post-colonial society. And that is true. Or that they are the problems of poverty and under-development. And that is true too. And South Africa's problems are those created by apartheid. One can say all sorts of true things about the predicament we are in; each science in fact has its own truth to tell. But if we want to know the truth about the predicament in order to overcome it then only philosophy can help us. The sciences and their technologies can provide us with the means to help us to a new South Africa but they cannot tell us what that newness should consist in. They cannot tell us what will bring our human nature to fulfilment, and what the real barriers to this fulfilment are.

In a nutshell, philosophy can help us in two ways. By giving us its own understanding of human nature it can help us understand our predicament, see how we have got into it and hence how to get out. It can also give us an insight into what kind of life is suitable for human persons and what qualities of character and kinds of institution this will require. In science we must work from the particular to the general: look at the problem, look for its causes, develop a hypothesis as to its solution, test the hypothesis for success. But of course this presupposes some criterion of success. It also presupposes some standard by virtue of which the problem is a problem. It even assumes some initial informal description of the problem that will guide it in its search for causes. If we are to question these presuppositions and assumptions we must turn to philosophy; and to avoid such assumptions and presuppositions philosophy must work from the general to the particular, from a consideration of human nature to a consideration of South Africa. I now propose to give some substance to these general remarks.

The origin of idolatry

From the outline of a philosophical conception of humanity given above it is possible to work out a general form of the human predicament as such. It is this: we have natural desires that our natural powers are insufficient to fulfill. The desires, being natural, are so imperious that we nevertheless attempt to fulfill them anyway. The resulting situation, being unable to satisfy us, constitutes our predicament.

Let me give this abstract formula some content. This is provided by our account of the necessary conditions for personal growth. We desire personal community with other persons. This is only possible if we develop those powers that make us persons. We can only do this if other persons take the initiative and offer themselves to personal community with us. We need other persons if our desire for personal community is to find fulfilment. If this desire is not fulfilled it will produce in us all sorts of desperate and misguided attempts to find fulfilment. These efforts will produce an interpersonal situation (together with all the surrounding effects that that will cause) that is the enemy of any human fulfilment, and which constitutes the concrete predicament we struggle to overcome.

Human beings are peculiar in this: they have a natural desire for something their natural powers are insufficient to achieve. We need community with others, but we can't get it unless it is given us by them. We want love but we can't acquire it by our own efforts; if it is not freely given us then it is not love that we receive.

This need for other persons is natural. It arises from the basic structure of human nature as I have set it out above. We have a natural capacity for self-realisation. But we are only able to exercise and develop this capacity if we are empowered by the influence of others; we are self-realising and other-dependent, and dependent on others for our self-realisation. There is something paradoxical about this formula to be sure, but it is a paradox that truly expresses what it is to be a human person.

This being the case it is not difficult to see why our attempts to find fulfilment should take the form of the creation of an illusory self-sufficiency. Seeking self-affirmation instinctively, it is perhaps inevitable to try to avoid all dependence on others and attempt to achieve it by self-assertion. Desiring community with others so much, it is perhaps inevitable to attempt to create it by dominating or controlling them.

The project of self-realisation is carried out at two levels, the social and the natural. As persons (self-realising beings) we need other persons as persons, for their own sake, and so our project of self-realisation takes the form of forming various associations with others, associations which embody a meaning or importance with which we seek wholly to identify. We are Nazis, or Jews, or Catholics, or whatever. As bodily beings (other-dependent) we are threatened by sickness and death, and need to fit in with our material environment. So we must seek to control it too, to make it provide food and clothing and shelter, health, security and the means of personal development, to control it as completely as possible.

It is important to see why our attempts at self-sufficiency are so all-consuming. Genuine personal growth consists in the growth of self-knowledge and self-affirmation. But genuine self-knowledge depends on being affirmed by one who already possesses it (as we saw in the previous chapter). If I do not remain open to this influence of other persons the knowledge I develop of myself is illusory. Nevertheless, desiring to affirm myself whole-heartedly, I come to whole-heartedly affirm the illusory image I have of myself. My heart is not in fact whole but riddled with conflicts; I nevertheless give my false self-image an unlimited or unconditional consent. Being self-realising entails a kind of unlimitedness in that it involves a certain transcendence of the limiting influences of external causes. There is thus in persons a psychic dynamism towards an unconditional or unlimited affirmation or commitment, a desire for something of unlimited or absolute value. It is this desire, not being satisfied, that presses us into an absolute commitment to a particular self-image, an absolute loyalty to a particular group, and a desire for absolute control over our material environment.

Post Hegelian philosophers such as Feuerbach, Marx and Sartre recognise this dimension of human existence, though each has their own explanation of it. And so do many writers in the human sciences, especially in psychology. It is also given religious expression in the Judaeo-Christian religious tradition in the idea of idolatry. Although the idol is always something other than the self it is worshipped for the sake of the power it is supposed to have, to save or satisfy the worshipper. In fact all the power it has, has been given it by its worshippers, who have thus made themselves its slaves, impotent to realise what they most desire. The ultimate object of worship, so the prophetic critics of the Old Testament and the apostolic writers of the New imply, is the worshippers themselves as they understand themselves to be. Idolatry in the last resort is self-worship, giving oneself, or an self-constructed image of oneself, an absolute or unconditional value.

Erich Fromm, in his analysis of Marx's theory of alienation, uses the notion of idolatry as an explanatory analogy that chimes in with what I am saying. "The whole concept of alienation found its first expression in Western thought in the Old Testament concept of idolatry. The essence of what the prophets call 'idolatry' is not that man worships many gods instead of only one. It is that the idols are the work of man's own hands – they are things, and man bows down and worships things; worships that which he has created himself. In doing so he transforms himself into a thing. He transfers to the things of his creation the attributes of his own life, and instead of experiencing himself as the creating person, he is in touch with himself only by the worship of the idol. He has become estranged from his own life forces, from the wealth of his own potentialities, and is in touch with himself only in the indirect way of submission to life frozen in the idols" (1961:44).

The twentieth-century idol

I have tried to show how this tendency towards absolute self-assertion derives from the basic structure of human nature as revealed by philosophical reflection. One cannot of course say that it is a necessary consequence of being human; because human beings are self-realising they are free to resist this pressure. Nevertheless, in view of the actual state of human individuals and communities in every known society, knowledge of such a fundamental dynamism has great explanatory power. Already we have seen how one is able to predict the general way it will show itself in the various realms in which human life is necessarily lived: through an unconditional identification with particular groups and with particular systems of values and particular self-images. But one can say more. The typical result of such attempts at self-realisation through self-assertion is a progressive disruption of community at every level. All sorts of opposition and conflict are set up – between individuals, within families, between different groups, between the different genders and different races, between classes and nations. At the same time another kind of opposition and conflict is being developed. This is not so evident because it is within the individual; it is that progressive disintegration of the person that we have already described in some detail in our philosophical outline. I will not describe it again here.

In all this, what philosophy has helped us see is that beneath the particular forms of conflict and suffering that we experience in this or that part of the world, in Europe or in Africa, and the particular loyalties and ideologies that dominate people's lives, there is this intra- and inter-personal dimension with its own dynamism. And it is from this dimension that the real human energy emanates, to create or to destroy.

So far all that we have had to say is true of all people in every society in every place and time. What forms does this basic human predicament take in our own time and place, in the last part of the twentieth century, in South Africa? The abstract account we have given above is able to act as a clue, indicating where we are to look and what signs we are to deem important.

In fact the signs are fairly obvious and few would deny their importance; it is only when we have to say what they are signs of, that difficulties arise and people disagree. Surely it is not controversial to see the colossal development of science and technology over the last 150 years as the single most important factor determining the lives and culture of people, initially in Europe and now throughout the world. Science and technology have given a characteristic form both to our material environment and to our own self-understanding. They have also given a characteristic form to the project of self-realisation, and so to the predicament in which we find ourselves.

First of all, science has given us the idea that we can, in time, know everything there is to be known. We can have comprehensive understanding of the universe, including ourselves and our place in it. So we are masters of the universe, at least in this theoretical sense. Why should we not be masters in a practical sense as well? It is part of the scientific myth that the satisfaction of all our reasonable desires (including, perhaps, that of living for ever) is in principle within our power. At least for a favoured few. All we need is time to gain the necessary knowledge and develop the necessary technology. Did ever the desire for total control take a more impressive form?

It is at its most impressive when considered in relation to our materiality, our control of nature and natural processes, including those in our own bodies. Yet even here there are grounds for anxiety: in spite of our technology people die of starvation and diseases spread. Nor is this the result of a lack of technical resources. Humanity has reached the point where it has sufficient control over nature to feed, clothe, house and give medical care to everyone in the world. Even the problem of communication and distribution could be overcome. The reason that it does not happen is a moral reason and not a practical one. Humanity cannot agree to do it.

This fact points to the connection between human disunity and the inability to control nature. Even if it is in principle possible for humanity to control nature, it is only possible if we are able to control ourselves and so agree to do so. As far as the scientific myth is concerned this is not an insuperable problem. In one sense the myth is right. If one is thinking of just any kind of control then there is no reason why a small group of Europeans (and Japanese and Americans) with the right kind of technology shouldn't completely control the rest of humanity. One way of doing this would be to liquidate them. If however we are thinking of ourselves as persons, as free beings, and of control as the strictly personal control of persons, then the problem of control suddenly exceeds the range of science. It becomes the problem of agreement, of solidarity, of community. And the truth is that we have not solved that problem, the problem of humanity's self-control; what is being shown us now is that until we do we shall not be able to control nature, or satisfy humanity's material needs, either.

Idolatry and ideology

We nevertheless proceed on the assumption that we can, with the result that the different kinds of opposition and conflict we have identified are given their contemporary form: between people and groups, within each individual, and between the whole of humanity and nature too. The most spectacular example of this is the ever-growing gap between the developed and the undeveloped nations. But the difficulty of marriage and family life in an affluent industrialised society is another. So is the progressive despoiling and pollution of the environment. And there are many more.

Together with the actual divisive and oppressive social structures created by our attempts at self-realisation through self-assertion, structures which take very various economic, legal and political forms (not to mention military ones), there are systems of ideas or ideologies which develop as a justification of the dominant practice, and a way of giving meaning and value to the lives of those involved.

There are very many such ideologies at work in the contemporary world. I will give idealised descriptions of just two that are representative of the full range of the ideological spectrum. They are not intended to conform precisely to the manifesto of any particular group, but rather to represent the kind of view of human life and fulfilment that a scientific and technological culture produces. I will call them the liberal and the socialist ideologies.

As its name implies, the liberal ideology is based on the value of freedom. Freedom however is understood in an individualistic way as being free of the power of others. People should be free to do as they please except only insofar as their decisions might interfere with the attempts of others to do as they please. Apart from that rule there are no others; morality is essentially a matter of private taste. The aim of public authorities is to organise and control the social system in such a way that this non-interference is maximised. The rules they make are essentially limitations on the freedom of individuals, but limitations which have the effect of reducing conflict of interest to a minimum. Some forms of liberalism require the rules to be authorised by some form of agreement between those subject to them; others recognise that some rules are objectively better than others because they have "stood the test of time", or are part of "common sense" or reflect the present scientific understanding of "human nature". The ultimate motive proposed to the individual for accepting and obeying the rules is enlightened self-interest. There is no conviction that the individual should desire the common good for its own sake, or that social harmony actually depends on shared values.

The socialist ideology sees society itself as the source of the value, freedom and rights of the individual. Because all that is of value in human life – even (for some versions of this ideology) our humanity itself – is derived from society, society's continued existence and stability is the highest value. For this reason society, understood as a system of institutions, takes precedence over the individual in a moral sense. In practice this usually means that the individual has no rights against the state. Because everything individuals have comes to them from society, including their legitimate desires, the problem of politics is simply that of educating individuals in such a way that they will all want the same thing, the continued existence and security of the state.

It can easily be seen that these two ideologies are in many ways simply two sides of the same coin. Neither subjects the authority of the state to any objective norm. They appear to be very different; each stresses one aspect of human nature to the exclusion of the other: liberalism our freedom from others, socialism our dependence on our social milieu. In fact however they are merely different forms of a materialist misunderstanding of human nature.

Socialism is clearly materialist: there is no sense in which persons transcend their social milieu; they are dependent on it for all they have and are, and can be conditioned to make it their own supreme value. A combination of scientific expertise and bureaucratic management is sufficient to organise society for the fulfilment of all its members needs.

But so too, despite appearances, is liberalism. The freedom of the individual is understood in purely negative terms, as something achieved by escaping the influence of others. The more I am subject to the other's influence, the less free I am; the more my behaviour is determined by the influence of the other, the less it is my own. This is the logic of materialism, best exemplified by the laws of the physical sciences, but generalised to include the world of persons as well.

Genuine human freedom however, as I have described it above, is a positive characteristic of human nature whereby each person has the capacity for self-realisation through self-knowledge and self-affirmation. This is a freedom that persists, and can even be enhanced, through dependence on others, because it is a power that is not limited in any way (though it could be rendered inoperative) by the action of external forces, and hence is incommensurable with the free influence of others.

Both ideologies typically claim to affirm the value of freedom, but the term is used equivocally, neither usage doing justice to true human freedom. The freedom valued by liberalism is the individual's freedom from non-interference. The freedom promised by socialism is the freedom of social harmony. In South Africa the liberal ideology predominates among the white group while the socialist predominates among the black. As our account of the necessary conditions for personal growth shows, however, true individual freedom of self-realisation is only possible by virtue of a certain kind of dependence on others. And social harmony that is a genuine solidarity of persons, rather than an engineered order that is sub-personal, depends for its existence on the individual freely affirming others and entering into community with them.

The notion of freedom itself is a "site of struggle" in present-day Africa. It is at the centre of discussion about the nature of the contemporary situation in Africa as a whole, or in this or that African country. It is also a concept that is at the heart of the understanding of persons I have developed in this book. And it is certainly one that stands in need of philosophical analysis.

In our context the most important distinction relating to the idea of freedom is that between individual and social freedom.

Individual freedom refers in the first place to the capacity for free action possessed by human individuals by virtue of their being subjects and persons. It is a transcendence of total determination by external causes, whether social or natural, of the kind discoverable by the sciences. It also denotes the condition of psychic integration in persons that is achieved by the proper development of this capacity. Such integration of the cognitive, volitional and emotional systems of the self enables one to commit oneself wholeheartedly to what one really wants to do, and constitutes the positive freedom of self-realisation.

Social freedom, on the other hand, is the lack of opposition and conflict between individuals or groups. Whenever there is opposition and conflict, the ability of those involved, whether individuals or groups, to realise themselves fully is impaired. The scope of activity of each is limited by the other. And always there is domination and subjection involved as well. The dominated group or individual is obviously deprived of freedom. But so is the dominator; the effort that could be used in positive self-expression is wasted in subjecting the other. In such a situation the mutuality and reciprocity, that are the features of genuine community between persons, are missing. It is thus only when the relations between individuals and groups are such as to foster individual freedom, that genuine social freedom exists as a positive state.

Thus freedom or liberation in the full sense can only occur when the conditions for personal growth and community are realised in the society in question. In contemporary Africa, because of its history of colonialism, freedom and liberation are often understood solely in a political, or even, on occasion, in a purely military, sense. This is a serious mistake. Freedom, or the lack of it, understood in a fully human way, affects every aspect of life. Philosophy also has a role to play in trying to relate the necessary conditions for human freedom to each different sphere of life, so as to help determine appropriate institutions and practices in that sphere. I now propose to consider the South African context of this comprehensive struggle for liberation.

Chapter Ten

The South African Context

I have tried to show how opposition between people and groups, as well as conflict within individuals, gets produced by our compulsive attempts to achieve self-realisation through self-assertion. This internal dynamism towards self-worship which produces different forms of idolatry is the ultimate cause of social oppression and personal disintegration. Our philosophical account of human nature and the conditions for personal growth show why this should be so.

A struggle of ideas

Together with the actual psychological and social conflict there are also produced systems of ideas: self-images, political ideologies, symbols of value – that explain, support and justify what happens. These systems always embody inadequate and mistaken conceptions of humanity.

I have begun to examine the contemporary African predicament by looking at the basic First World/Third World opposition which is an opposition in terms of both technological and cultural resources, including scientific know-how. I have also sketched a picture of the dominant ideologies that go with this state of affairs, the liberal and the socialist.

The primary sphere in which philosophy can be of help in contemporary Africa is the sphere of ideologies and value-systems. It can do this not only by providing a method by means of which people can become more conscious and critical of these systems of ideas, but also by providing a more adequate conception of humanity on which to base one's value judgments and one's political programmes.

I am convinced that this is the most important dimension of the struggle that is at present going on between the developed and the undeveloped nations of the world. It is a struggle to develop and give expression to a new way of being human, different from what is presented by European culture as it spreads across the globe, and different too no doubt from that realised by the "primitive" cultures of the past. A colleague who thinks the same as I do on this matter has put this so well that I will simply quote from him.

"The unity of the human race has at last become as inescapable a fact of experience as its racial and cultural diversity. But it is still, manifestly, a very imperfect and shadowy unity. And more to the point though less commonly remarked upon, it is the result of a stupendously energetic and partly deliberate, partly unconscious, European cultural imperialism.

Now what we are observing at the present moment, since the end of the Second World War in 1945, to be precise, is an increasingly determined reaction all over the world against this cultural imperialism and against Americo-European cultural hegemony. In my opinion the division of the world on the so-called North-South lines, or of Third World against First and Second Worlds, is of far more momentous significance than the division between the Western, free-enterprise capitalist world and the Eastern, Marxist socialist one, that so obsesses Washington and Moscow and their respective satellites. This conflict gets more like the rivalry between opposing *magna latrocinia*, great bands of robbers, as St. Augustine termed any state or empire which is constituted without justice. Each side represents some aspect of the degradation, the corruption by power of European culture; a degradation that can be summed up in the word, 'materialism'; a preoccupation with things, with objects, a valuing of things and above all of the thing of things, money, more than people ....

It is indeed where we have a confrontation between the other cultures of the world and the American-European culture complex, whether of the First or of the Second World brand, that we have more genuine questions of value involved. I am not talking about the confrontation of Third World governments and the West, or the East. Many of these are as corrupt and unjust as any in the world – *parva latrocinia*. I am talking rather about what is going on in the Third World itself, below government level, and also in the immigrant ghettos of Europe and the United States. It is a shapeless, un-co-ordinated, un-thought-out, but all the same spontaneous and persistent resistance to European *hubris*. For all its limitations and apparent ineffectiveness it is there, and what it is saying is that there are other ways of being human, in many respects better and more humane ways than the materialist ones which are what comes across as the

American-European-Russian way of being human. It is an assertion of the real value of cultural diversity which in no way rejects the actual geopolitical unity that is a modern fact of life, but resists the pressure to turn it into a uniformity. Some material uniformity there is bound to be, some world-wide cultural assimilation. There is the uniformity of the jeans-Coke-football world culture (to which, alas, one can add the uniformity of the arms trade).

But I cannot help feeling that it is only Third World resistance to European cultural imperialism which can save us from the world-wide cultural impoverishment of sheer reduction to the level of these lowest common denominators. It is Third World conceptions of humanity that can, paradoxically, preserve for us the truly humane cultural treasures of the very rich European tradition" (Hill, 1984:189–192).

This new conception of humanity, together with the new social and cultural forms in which it can be expressed, will be produced to cope with the situation of conflict between European culture and technology as it spreads across the globe and the rest of the world. And of course it must be constructed out of the materials that are there engaged, that is to say European ideas as well as those emanating from the local cultures. Senghor is right to point us towards a "civilisation of the universal" and to see it as the result of "cultural miscegenation", of the merging of traditions in which different traditions of thought are complementary to each other. The merging is, however, no automatic process but a struggle, like the economic and the political struggles but on the level of intellect and feeling. The attempt I have made above to give systematic philosophical expression to a conception of humanity that gives a central place to traditional African ideas as well as retaining the integrity of an important European philosophical tradition, is intended as a contribution to this.

African ideas

An indication of the road and the direction in which philosophy will have to travel in a South African context is given by the African philosophers I have already referred to, particularly those like Senghor who recognise the contribution that traditional African thought has to make to a future synthesis with a European culture that is here to stay.

The African predicament is seen in much the same terms as I have used, as "a world dominated by Whites, in a socio-cultural context marked by racialism, slavery and colonialism, in an economic situation of underdevelopment and in a political condition which is continuously threatened by upheavals from within and by neo-colonialism from without" (Ruch & Anyanwu, 1984:20). In this context Senghor's negritude is an attempt at "reforging the unity of man and the world by linking the flesh to the spirit, man to fellow man, the pebble to God" (1939:314). The three crucial elements that traditional African thought has to offer a future "civilisation of the universal" are the idea of vital force as the foundation of reality, that of the dialectical connection between spirit and matter, and the vision of communal society which is "rather a communion of souls than an aggregate of individuals" (1965:49).

The various attempts in post-colonial Africa to embody elements such as these in one or other form of "African socialism" are well known. By some African thinkers, Mammadou Dia for instance, this is seen explicitly as an attempt to effect "a synthesis between individualistic and socialistic values" (Apostel, 1981: 388). Apostel quotes Dia: "This synthesis of a true socialism and a true humanism, which will rest on African reality and African values while not rejecting the enriching contributions of other cultures, will be genuinely African, but at the same time have universal importance" (1981:388). Over the years there has developed a characteristic African ideology. Apostel describes this in the following terms: "an egalitarian, co-operative, collectivistic welfare state in which however, simultaneously, the autonomy and dignity of man (the *muntu*) is maximalised" (1981:386).

Ruch distinguishes three elements in a typically "African" ideology: national unity, communalism, and development on a human scale.

Colonialism disrupted the tribal system, but imposed a certain unity on society. Independence saw the creation of an artificial unity in a new nation. Tribal unities no longer exist, so a single-party state is required to focus the loyalties of the population. The ideal of government of such a state is consensus democracy, with a lot of grassroots participation in decision-making. Organisation will be non-bureaucratic as far as possible, striving to retain the "familyhood" of traditional society.

Communalism, the second element in this ideology, is a kind of socialism, but is sharply opposed to any socialism of a European kind, especially Marxism. It is to be seen rather as an up-dating of the traditional emphasis on community as an ethical and religious ideal. Communal elements, such as the non-individual ownership of land and other co-operative and egalitarian institutions, exist for their own sake and not as a means to economic progress. Communalism implies above all, a quality of life made possible by common attitudes and loyalties. It is not something that can be achieved simply by legislation. In the last resort it is something that cannot exist without a religious justification and support. A successful society that is not religious through and through is unthinkable in an African context. On the other hand, as we shall see, traditional African religion is not separated from political life as has come to be the case in Europe and the First World. God, in African traditional thought, has a very human face and is very much at home in the human world.

Development on a human scale has many aspects to it. Here I will mention just two: planned poverty, and the solidarity of nations.

The African economist Tevoedjre has made the former expression famous in his book *Poverty, the Wealth of Mankind*. His idea is that Africa must go her own economic way, not copy from the First of Second Worlds; planned poverty is "a democratic conception in which a country makes the option in favour of poverty for each one and of the greatest possible wealth for all" (1979:121). I do not intend to go into the details of this plan. Basically it is an attempt to avoid wastage, and to prevent material production and consumption from becoming the goal of society, to the detriment of the human quality of life. It is a search for simplicity in the life of society rather than the proliferation of artificial needs which is the present glory of the West.

The idea of the solidarity of nations is one that emanates very naturally from Africa. It is the extension of the idea of familyhood on a global scale. One expression of it is Senghor's "Civilisation of the Universal". But it also has a strong economic logic to it: Africa needs and will continue to need the help, especially the scientific and technological help, of the rest of the world. As Apostel puts it, "All Africa feels itself as composed of have-nots, and class-struggle, not denied, is seen not as a national but an international entity; the gradual reduction of material foreign aid on a large scale in favour of technological and educational assistance in order to enhance the human quality of African work, is both a rational move towards independence and an expression of African philosophy" (1981:387).

This sketch of how African thinkers see the contemporary predicament of Africa, how African ideas may help to overcome it, and the way in which we ought to move, can serve as an introduction to our consideration of our own situation in South Africa.

The South African context

In South Africa the opposition between people and groups of people set up by inauthentic attempts at self-realisation assumes symbolic perfection in apartheid. The concept of apartheid refers both to the actual social situation in South Africa and to the ideology that explains and justifies it.

With regard to the social system we have first of all, as in the rest of Africa, a relic of colonialism. There is a difference however; in South Africa the First World has not retired from the Third but remains in the midst of it. Some have called this "internal" colonialism: a small First World group controlling a large Third World population that is economically dependent on it. The group-opposition in South Africa does not however end there. In South Africa the small First World group has all the political and military power. So there is an opposition between the rulers and the ruled as well as between those with resources and those without. This is more or less the opposition between white and non-white, though some non-whites have more political power of a delegated kind than others. At any rate the degree of political power depends on race. In addition to this there is a constructed political opposition between the different black language-groups, each being assigned its separate "homeland" and "independent" political status. Within the "motherland" there is the opposition of designated groups of "white", "coloured" and "indian". Apart from all these officially created and recognised oppositions there are a host of less easily defined others. There is an opposition of a kind between English- and Afrikaans-speaking white groups, as well as the normal oppositions of different political parties, and the opposition between owners and workers, and all the other particular oppositions that one would find in other First and Third World settings. In all this landscape of opposition there is however the one dramatic divide that has made South Africa a paradigm of separation and given it its symbolic stature: the division between white and non-white (these terms are carefully chosen as being more in keeping with the spirit of apartheid) is the focus for all the other important divisions as well, of power, resources, military strength and so on. All the oppositions in South Africa get their distinctive character from this. A look at the ideological content of apartheid will show why this is so.

I will follow Nolan's well-known analysis of the ideology of apartheid, in distinguishing within the concept four elements: racism, capitalism, nationalism and the idea of the national security state (Nolan,1989). To this I add the element of religion.

1. Racism. The European colonist in South Africa saw the non-European peoples of Africa as inferior to them in all sorts of ways, but particularly with regard to civilization and culture. In addition to the original enslavement of numbers of the local population, they gradually created a feudal society over much of South Africa as they (in particular the Afrikaner *voortrekkers*) opened up the interior for European farming.

2. Capitalism. The discovery of gold and diamonds in South Africa towards the end of the nineteenth century produced an industrial revolution in South Africa after the model of that in Europe. It had the same effect as in Europe, the creation of two classes, the owners of the means of production and those who were needed to work them. In South Africa however the workers were all black. The gold was very deep underground and white miners were reluctant to mine it. There were many more black workers available, and they would work for much lower wages. The owners of the mines were of course white.

3. Nationalism. After the war between the Afrikaner republics and the British, Afrikaner nationalism developed apace in an attempt to compete with the economic and political power of the English who were in control of the mines and the government. Its success, first in the political and then in the economic fields, gradually reinforced the racism and the capitalism already in existence. The policy of "separate development" and the official designation of different "nations" each with its separate homeland, fitted in well both with the racist desire not to mingle with inferior peoples and with the capitalist need for labour without too much responsibility for the labour force. Homeland "citizens" were always available as migrant labour, while remaining the ultimate responsibility of their own homeland governments.

4. The national security state. Like many other Third World countries (Brazil, Argentina, Uruguay, Paraguay, Chile, Taiwan, South Korea and the Philippines) the economically powerful class, together with the military, has come together on the basis of opposition to "communism". The state is given great power and exercises total control over every aspect of society through the "security" forces, including the police. The idea of security becomes an absolute value, and society is divide into a small "secure" elite and a huge marginalised rootless mass.

5. Religion. The ideology of apartheid received theological justification from the Calvinist Dutch Reformed Churches to which most Afrikaners belonged. From the early days of colonialism the fact that Christianity was

part of European culture contributed to the assumption of European superiority. The idea of a Christian missionary effort in South Africa also helped justify colonial expansion.

The Calvinist notion of "orders of creation" was used, together with a fundamentalist reading of the Bible, to produce a theory of separate nations as part of God's plan. This fitted well the political programme of separate development in separate "homelands".

In spite of the opposition of most Christian denominations and other religions to apartheid, the actual separation of racial groups imposed by the system led to racial segregation even in these congregations. As a result break-away groups began to form who accepted the separation and proclaimed themselves "black" churches. A huge number of African independent churches has grown up in which elements of Christianity and Judaism and traditional African religion are combined. And there are certain movements in Islam that present Islam as a religion for "black" people.

The ideology of apartheid and the institutions that embody it have so dominated South Africa that an intense spiritual climate of group identity and absolute group loyalty has been created. The idea of identity-in-separation affects everyone, not just the supporters of apartheid. A real difficulty of human communication between groups is the result. This causes difficulty of communication between those of the same group as well; a common identity based on opposition and hostility is no medium for a full and open sharing of life. The pattern of idolatry – self-assertion through absolute commitment to ideologies and groups – is perfectly realised in South Africa. This is one reason why the struggle for a more just and peaceful society in South Africa is so significant, even for other places in the world that are not really involved.

If the separation and opposition I have described is the most fundamental barrier to personal growth and community, it is of course not the only one. Apartheid has other inhuman and dehumanising characteristics and effects, many of which, such as avoidable poverty, deprivation of political power, marginalisation of large numbers, unemployment, corruption and brutalisation of the police force and army, increase of crime and mindless consumerism, are shared by most Third-World countries and exist in First World countries too. Some aspects of our predicament however seem to stand out with revelatory clarity and deserve closer attention.

In South Africa all the forms of opposition are affected by the fundamental opposition between white and black. So the effects of the predicament on individuals are characterised by which side of this fundamental divide one lives. For example, it is possible to use the concept of alienation to describe the effects of apartheid on people, but the typical forms of alienation will be significantly different for black and white. Whites are alienated from blacks by seeing them simply as functionaries; blacks are alienated from whites by seeing them as monsters of inhumanity. Whites are alienated from themselves by an inauthentic sense of shame and guilt; blacks from themselves by an inauthentic shame at their impotence and blackness. I will be looking at this in some detail presently.

In general one can say that the system of apartheid produces a state of chronic fear, anxiety and guilt-feeling, escapism and a break up of family-life. Whites fear a free society for that means a loss of control. Their anxiety is about security. The sense of guilt derives from being identified with and the beneficiaries of an unjust and oppressive system. Escapism expresses itself in mindless leisure pursuits and consumerism. White South Africans have the highest divorce rate in the world.

Blacks fear the loss of freedom, or rather, to the degree to which they are already deprived of it, they hate it and fear its effects in their lives. Their anxiety is the anxiety of not being in control of their lives, the anxiety of impotence. Their sense of guilt attaches to their inability to change the unjust system, their acquiescence in it, their preferring to feather a private nest to working for the common good. Escapism takes the form of mindless violence and various forms of drugging. Personal intimacy between married couples is rare, and parental control of children is almost impossible.

The vices of a particular society tend to be the vices of the dominant class and culture, and in South Africa this is that of the whites. The mode of self-assertion that affects all of society and its institutions, the dominant idolatry, is that which we have described above, namely the idolatry of science and technology as the providers of total understanding and control. It is the mistaken conception of human nature and human flourishing and fulfilment derived from this that has produced our predicament.

For the struggle against apartheid to be the struggle for a genuine humanity, the conception of the humanity (and the humane institutions) we hope for is all-important. It would be spiritual suicide to assume that the only alternatives are the current European ideologies on offer – capitalism or communism, liberalism or socialism. If we want to build a society that will last we must build with local materials. In the light of what I have argued thus far it ought to be possible to show the relevance of an African conception of humanity for the struggle against apartheid.

Surely there can be no doubt that, whatever its special characteristics, the apartheid system is part of the global conflict created by the spread of European culture and technology across the world. It is not indeed the technological power as such that is the problem, but the conception of humanity that goes with it, and the values that stem from that. It is these values that determine how that power is applied and in whose interests it is used.

The aim of the struggle against apartheid is not a society in which everyone will enjoy the level of consumption of goods and services that a small minority now enjoys, or the freedom to make as much money as we can. Nor is it a society in which ideological uinformity and orthodoxy is achieved by a centralised bureaucracy, so that all aspects of life are controlled by a single system of ideas (albeit a new one), and the planners and so-called experts that implement them. In both cases humanity is sacrificed to fundametally inhuman systems and to forces that are de-humanising.

Whether one is thinking of the forces of the free market or the forces of bureaucracy and ideology, one is thinking of a kind of force that does not reach the properly personal level – the level or *seriti*. Any society that sacrifices the personal influence of persons on other persons, or tries to find some substitute for it, will end up a dehumanising one. Social control is necessary; so is individual freedom. But the right measure for each can only be determined by something still more fundamental: a true understanding of our need to be in personal touch with other persons, and the kinds of milieu in which genuinely personal powers can flourish. Our social institutions must respect this need and create this milieu.

The idol of apartheid

In spite of recent changes the struggle for human liberation in South Africa is still the struggle against the idol of apartheid and its continuing power in our midst. Apartheid is such a perfect example of the human predicament, its character and causes, as I have come to depict in this book, that I want to dwell a little longer on it and subject it to further analysis. To my mind a great deal of light is thrown on the nature of apartheid by the work of the French philosopher Simone Weil.

As far as I know this is the first application of Weil's ideas to the South African situation, and is surely long overdue. Weil was exiled to England during the occupation of France and, while there, asked by the Free French to set down her ideas concerning the reconstruction of French society after the war. The parallels with post-apartheid South Africa are striking, and Weil's work is a model of the application of philosophy to concrete human and social issues.

Our philosophical account of the necessary conditions for personal growth showed that human persons are completely dependent on their environment. especially their environment of other persons, for their development and fulfilment as persons. This truth about persons is expressed by Simone Weil in terms of a need for roots. "To be rooted is perhaps the most important and least recognized need of the human soul. It is one of the hardest to define ... Every human being needs to have multiple roots. It is necessary for him to draw well nigh the whole of his moral, intellectual and spiritual life by way of the environment of which he forms a natural part" (1952:41).

She goes on to define roots in the following way: "A human being has roots by virtue of his real, active and natural participation in the life of a community which preserves in living shape certain particular treasures of the past and certain particular expectations for the future" (1952:41). She uses this idea of our need for roots to analyse the effect that enemy occupation would have on the people of France, and to suggest ways in which French society could be rebuilt and morale restored after the war, analysing the Frech predicament in terms of "uprootedness", and prescribing as remedy "the growing of roots".

I have noted the parallel with the South African situation. There are differences to be sure, but there is a parallel between the German occupation of France and the rule of apartheid in South Africa. And Weil has managed to reveal the universal character of her conception of a need for roots, uprootedness and the growing of roots. It is most instructive to make an application of what she says to our own situation today.

She lists a variety of causes of uprootedness. Describing the causes gives concrete content to the idea of roots itself.

First, there is military conquest by a foreign power. The uprooting effects of conquest are most extreme when the conquerors remain in the conquered territory but are not assimilated to the local culture. Examples of this are the Germans themselves, and the French and British in their colonies. And there is a clear parallel with South Africa even now.

Secondly, even without a military conquest, "money-power and economic domination can so impose a foreign influence as actually to provoke this disease of uprootedess" (1952:42). Contemporary examples of this are First World multinational companies in the Third World, and foreign aid to underdeveloped countries.

Thirdly, the domination of money in the lives of workers also has an uprooting effect. The life of a worker is reduced solely to its wage-earning potential. Workers in factories and mines are like immigrants in a foreign country, quite separated from the environment in which they grew up and learnt to feel at home in the world. And unemployment is "uprootedness raised to the second power" (1952:43).

Fourthly, modern education is a most important cause of uprootedness, both as regards its methods and as regards its content. As regards its content, "strongly directed towards and influenced by technical science, very strongly tinged with pragmatism, extremely broken up by specialization" (1952:43), it effects a complete break with the traditional culture as well as with the rest of life, especially with values. As regards the way in which education is administered in modern society, its effect is to separate an educated "elite" from the rest of society. The distinction between the educated and uneducated becomes a mere socio-economic one, and not at all the distinction between the wise and the foolish.

Fifthly, all kinds of migratory labour are an obvious cause of uprootedness, especially when, as in South Africa, wives or husbands and families of the worker are not permitted to live with them. This form of uprootedness can be linked to that caused by the move to the cities that is so characteristic of an industrialised society, especially in the Third World. The culture and morality of the countryside is often left behind there; it does not seem to fit the new circumstances of life on the margins of a city.

Sixthly, there is colonialism, a cause of uprootedness that is of special interest to us. Weil draws attention to "the terrible uprootedness which European colonial methods always produce."(1952:49) Speaking of the depopulation of the countryside in favour of the cities, she describes it as a disease "that the white man carries about with him wherever he goes. The disease has even penetrated into the heart of the African continent, which had for thousands of years, nevertheless, been made up of villages. These black people at any rate, when nobody came to massacre them, torture them, or reduce them to slavery, knew how to live happily on their land. Contact with us is making them lose the art" (1952:77).

Seventhly, there is a certain kind of rapid social change or revolution. One kind of revolution consists in the transformation of society in such a way that the workers are given roots in it; the other consists in spreading the rootlessness of the working-class to the whole of society. Weil makes the point that the second kind of revolution is more common. This is because uprootedness either produces apathy or violence; thus when the uprooted act, they act vioently to uproot others. She gives as examples the Germans (who "at the time Hitler assumed command over them were really ... a nation of proletarians, that is to say, uprooted individuals" (1952:45) and the Romans, who "were a handful of fugitives who banded themselves together artificially to form a city, and deprived the Mediterranean peoples of their individual manner of life, their country, traditions, past history to such an extent that posterity has taken them, at their own valuation, for the founders of civilization in these conquered territories" (1952:45). Needless to say Simone Weil is no admirer of Roman "civilization".

Having put together this list it is not too difficult to see that what Simone Weil calls uprootedness is a direct result of the general economic, political, social and cultural changes that have occurred in Europe during the last half or the nineteenth century and the first half of the twentieth. South Africa has undergone similar changes in all these spheres of life during this period so it is not too difficult to apply the concept of uprootedness to our own situation.

Creating a nation

The principal form taken by uprooteness in social life is the obliteration of all natural and intermediate groupings by the nation-state. "For a long time now, the single nation has played the part which constitutes the supreme mission of society towards the individual human being, namely, maintaining throughout the present the links with the past and the future" (1952:95). The family, workers guilds, village, district, provincial communities no longer fulfill this role. Even the nation has lost its organic form and is defined now simply as "a territorial aggregate whose various parts recognise the authority of the same state" (1952:95). The state is the real unifying force in modern society and the unity it imposes on the life of society is essentially impersonal.

"The state is a cold concern which cannot inspire love, but itself kills, suppresses everything that might be loved" (1952:109). The modern state actually exists in opposition to the people it is supposed to serve. "The totalitarian phenomenon of the state arises through a conquest carried out by the public authorities of the people under their care" (1952:114). Consequently, because of this fundamental divide, the state cannot be the foundation for a citizen's identity, the object of their patriotic love.

Patriotism, in a broad sense, is the category under which Weil discusses the uprootedness of citizens in the modern nation-state. Overcoming uprootedness of this kind must be the organisation of society in such a way as to make true patriotism possible.

True patriotism can only be a loyalty and devotion to some limited, concrete community, a village, a province, a particular geographical region. It really is the expression of a sense of obligation beyond self-interest to "the public good" or "the common good". Weil defines one's country as one's "vital medium" (1952:154). So patriotism is really an extension of natural self-love and the desire for self-affirmation. This expresses itself in the readiness to sacrifice oneself for one's country and also in the ability to feel compassion for it. Thus true patriotism is the very opposite of jingoistic triumphalism. One will fight for one's country because it is threatened or oppressed, but not so that it can expand its empire or prestige. True patriotism shows itself especially in its compassion for the poorest of the country's people. "A patriotism inspired by compassion gives the poorest part of the population a privileged moral position" (1952:167).

By the time the Nazi army over-ran France, state control of the country had so alienated the people that true patriotism was impossible for most, the workers in particular. It was only through the destruction of the state by enemy occupation that the French rediscovered France; this was particularly true of those who, like Weil, went into exile. She writes, "All Frenchmen have come to feel the reality of France through being deprived of her" (1952:152). It may be that this is true of many, even most, South Africans. Most South Africans have never been able to identify completely with the country. There is even a sense in which the country as such, or the nation in a non-artificial sense, has not yet begun to exist. The state has been the ruler rather than the servant of the people and made them foreigners in their own land. "South Africa" is really still an idea for a future country. Nevertheless, the deprivation of a true homeland has given all South Africans a deep nostalgia and a strong hope for one. Whether it is possible to create a genuine nation out of so many disparate elements remains to be seen.

In spite of the totalitarian deformation of the state in modern societies, the state does have a genuine role to play. In Weil's words "The state's duty is to make the country, in the highest possible degree, a reality" (1952:157). One must remember Weil's definition of a country as "a vital medium". Although the state is the servant of the people, it has the highest responsibility of all because it is concerned with the total environment in which every individual is rooted and from which they must draw their life. Because of this the state has a kind of sacredness, though of an essentially symbolic kind. "This doesn't mean an idolizing of the state in association with patriotism in the Roman style. It is the exact opposite of this. The state is sacred, not in the way an idol is sacred, but in the way common objects serving a religious purpose, like the altar, the baptismal water or anything else of the kind , are sacred" (1952:173). She then points out that the only alternative to such an attitude to the state, and the nation that it serves, is either anarchy or idolatry, an idolatry of left or right; "in the language of today, the absence of a pure source of inspiration would leave the French people no other alternatives than anarchy, Communism or Fascism" (1952:1973).

In the light of this, obedience to public authorities becomes a serious obligation, subject only to the dictates of conscience. "A country cannot possess liberty unless it is recognised that disobedience towards the authorities, every time it doesn't proceed from an overriding sense of duty, is more dishonourable than theft" (1952:171). Public officials such as the police and civil servants should be chosen and trained with this in mind; they should be people who are worthy of respect. Judges, especially, should receive a moral and spiritual education as well as a legal one. They must be people who love the truth.

Weil is quite emphatic that unless one can reconstruct the administrative organs of society, and the form of its public life, on the basis of objective moral values rather than economic or political expediency, there is no hope for an ordered society in which citizens can grow new roots.

One might think that with this sketch of an ideal society Weil's study of the creation of a free France would be complete. But it is not; it is only half done. The other half, and the more important one, consists in getting people to realise the ideal. And this is the job of education, but education understood in the deepest and widest sense as moral education, the creation of a spirit in people's hearts that will enable them to follow where their minds would lead.

Education, understood in this sense, "whether its object be children or adults, individuals or an entire people, or even oneself – consists in creating motives. To show what is beneficial, what is obligatory, what is good – that is the task of education. Education concerns itself with the motives for effective action. For no action is ever carried out in the absence of motives capable of supplying the indispensable amount of energy for its execution. To want to direct human creatures – others or oneself – towards the good by simply pointing out the direction, without making sure the necessary motives have been provided, is as if one tried, by pressing down the accelerator, to set off in a motor-car with an empty petrol tank" (Weil 1952:181).

But how is one to discover and work on the motives that lie hidden in people's hearts? Through the conceptions, the ideals and ideologies (the idols), that determine their activities and give meaning to their lives. Such conceptions are only compatible with certain motives and not with others. The aim of education is to modify people's dominant conceptions in such a way as to foster the growth in their hearts of the love of what is perfect or best. All the energies and instruments of education should be subordinated to this end. "An educational method which is not inspired by the conception of a certain form of human perfection is not worth very much. When it is a matter of educating a whole people, the conception should be that of a civilization. It must not be sought in the past, which only contains imperfect models; far less still in dreams of the future which are necessarily as mediocre as we ourselves are, and consequently vastly inferior to the past. The inspiration for such an education must be sought, like the method itself, among the truths eternally inscribed in the nature of things" (1952:209). Weil supplies a detailed list of the "needs of the soul" that such an education ought to recognise and seek to satisfy. They amount to a concrete picture of our fundamental human nature that never varies (is "eternal") but underlies every form of society and which only philosophical wisdom (and no particular science) can discern.

Education of this kind is, as Socrates and Plato realised, a mysterious matter. Mere technical methods will not suffice. The person of the educator and the nature of the relation between the teacher and the pupil are all-important. Weil lists four obstacles to the development of this kind of education in contemporary society. They are a false conception of greatness as power, power over others and power to obtain pleasure; a degradation of the sentiment of justice to that of "law and order" or control; the idolization of money; the lack of religious inspiration.

These four obstacles have a common foundation: the scientific notion of power as physical force. This is such an all-pervasive notion in our culture that it determines our thinking far beyond the realm of physical science where it originated. Weil sees it as fundamentally opposed to all forms of genuine humanism, since it involves a reduction of specifically human energies to sub-human forces. Utilitarianism, economic liberalism and Marxism are all produced by applying this inadequate idea to different spheres of human life.

From the point of view of traditional African thought, Weil's critique of a materialistic idea of force is extremely interesting. She lacks the concept for a kind of force that would include both physical and spiritual aspects, but she certainly sees the need for it.

Her account of how education of the kind she feels is required could be provided, remains incomplete. Not only is the process of education itsef a problem, but the person of the educator is as well. Who is to do it? In view of her negative view of the state it would be quite mistaken, as well as unrealistic, to imagine the state generating this inspiration. It is perhaps unsurprising that, in her situation, the only agency she could think of was the Free French itself, in exile in London. What she has to say about them is of interest to us since it could be applied to our own liberation movements, such as the ANC.

One can sum up our description of the South African predicament by returning to the idea of community with which we began. South Africa has never had the kind of unity that is appropriate to a national group; apartheid has ensured that true human community hardly exists at any level. The present struggle has as its aim the establishing of the necessary conditions for this, political, economic and cultural in the broad sense. Can philosophy play a part in this?

A philosophical conception of humanity can help us in two ways. It can indicate spheres of life where sickness must be diagnosed and health produced. It can also identify values that ought to guide our aims at health, and standards that ought to control our efforts to achieve these. In the following two chapters I propose to do this, first in the sphere of work and then in that of gender relations.

Chapter Eleven

Work: Solidarity and Creativity

In each sphere of life a philosophy of persons can help us determine the ways in which the fundamental human predicament shows itself in that sphere. It can also help us to understand the particular sphere itself and the place and importance it has in human life as a whole, and to choose appropriate terms with which to describe it. Applying our account of the necessary conditions for personal growth and community to this description will enable us to derive more concrete and particular criteria for liberation in this realm. Finally these criteria can help us to envisage the changes in the practices, insitutions and methods that should be brought about.

In tackling the task of liberation one has always to keep in mind the connection between individual freedom of choice and social freedom from conflict and oppression. Personal growth depends on personal community with others, and vice versa. Hence true human liberation entails both inner and outer liberation, liberation of a psychic as well as a social kind.

The nature and importance of work

In our philosophy of persons we have distinguished two aspects: human persons are both self-realising and other-dependent. And we realise ourselves only through our dependence, on other persons firstly, but also on our impersonal environment as well. Work is the sphere of human life where the personal and the impersonal are most intimately connected. In the personal realm it involves the co-operation of persons in common work; in the impersonal realm it involves the transformation of the world by labour to make it a hospitable milieu for human life. Liberation in both these realms is needed if personal growth and community is to be achieved.

Work is the activity whereby we transform our environment for human use and development and make it a hospitable home for humanity. The nature and importance of work has been revealed as never before by the phenomenal development of science and technology since the beginning of the nineteenth century. We now have the knowledge and the power to fulfill the promise contained in the first sentence of this paragraph. If it doesn't happen, or happens only selectively, so that babies continue to die of starvation or contagious diseases to spread, then we have failed – and it is our fault.

When we speak of transforming our environment we are thinking of a bewildering variety of transformations of the same underlying material which nature provides: new tools, new means of communication, new sources of energy, new forms of food, medicine, housing, transport, instruments of learning and education. In such transformations we not only change our environment; in intimate interaction with it, we change ourselves.

In his classic work *Small is Beautiful* (which has the subtitle, "A study of economics as if people mattered"), Schumacher lists three functions of human work: "to give a man a chance to utilise and develop his faculties, to enable him to overcome his egocentredness by joining with other people in a common task, and to bring forth the goods and services needed for a becoming existence" (1973). As such a list shows, the centrality of work in human life is not merely accidental, an unfortunate historical development one should strive to supersede.

Work is central to human life because in it our whole nature is expressed, physical and spiritual elements combining in one integrated activity. Simone Weil, more than any other philosopher concerned with the sphere of work, has taught us to see it in this way. She follows Marx in seeing work as the crucial category for social analysis, but does so for a different reason. Marx chose the sphere of work for analysis because he believed economic factors determined all the rest. Weil chooses it because work is the place where thought and action, spiritual meaning and physical movement, come together most fully and typically. It is also the sphere where individuals are most dependent on co-operation and agreement with others if their projects are to be successful, and where the community depends most on the willing and intelligent participation of individuals.

"There thus emerges a new method of social analysis which is not that of Marx, although it starts, as Marx wanted, from the relationships of production; but whereas Marx ... seems to have wanted to classify the modes of production in terms of output, these would be analysed in terms of the relationships between thought and action" (1958:100). In other words, if one is to judge the forms and instruments of labour in a given society from the point of view of their compatibility with human freedom and development, then one has to take into account this intrinsic relation between the human elements of the activity itself, namely thought and choice and feeling. The concentration and discipline required of us in work are an important instrument of personal growth in us; the creativity involved can be such as to produce a meaning to life capable of expressing such growth. Providing the right conditions for work is thus one of the most important ways in which we can enable people to develop as persons to the full.

The centrality and importance of work in human life has been emphasized by a hundred year-old tradition of papal teaching in the Catholic Church, beginning with the pioneering encyclical of Leo XIII, *Rerum Novarum*, in 1891. This finds contemporary expression in John Paul II's *Laborem Exercens* (1981). There he reaffirms the teaching of this tradition that "human work has an ethical value of its own, which clearly and directly remains linked to the fact that the one who carries it out is a person, a conscious and free subject, that is to say, a subject that decides about himself" (1981:16). From this he draws the conclusion that the ultimate purpose of work is to be found in the producer rather than the product; as he puts it "work is 'for man' and not man 'for work'" (1981:17).

This idea, that it is the worker rather than the product that is the most important part of work, and the factor that ought to carry most weight in deciding what work is to be done and how it is to be done, also finds powerful expression in the writings of Simone Weil, who is a prophetic figure in this sphere of human life in the twentieth century.

Because of the colossal development of science and technology, our ability to transform and to "humanise" the world of nature has been immeasurably increased. Because of this Weil thinks that the twentieth century "has a peculiar mission, or vocation – the creation of a civilization founded on the spiritual nature of work" (1952:91). She speaks as the prophet of such a civilization: "A civilization based upon the spirituality of work would give to man the very strongest possible roots in the wide universe, and would consequently be the opposite of that state in which we now find ourselves, characterized by an almost total uprootedness" (1952:94).

This "spirituality of work" is based on the fact that work is the most common and comprehensive form taken by that "dying in order to live" that is the principle of all genuinely personal growth. "Physical labour is a daily death. To labour is to place one's own being, body and soul, in the circuit of inert matter, turn it into an intermediary between one state and another of a fragment of matter, make of it an instrument. The labourer turns his body and soul into an appendix of the tool which he handles. The movements of the body and the concentration of the mind are a function of the requirements of the tool, which is itself adapted to the matter being worked upon" (1952:286).

And she continues: "The world only gives itself to man in the form of food and warmth if man gives himself to the world in the form of labour. But death and labour can be submitted to either in an attitude of revolt or in one of consent. They can be submitted to either in their naked truth or else wrapped around with lies ... Immediately next in order after consent to suffer death, consent to the law which makes work indispensable for conserving life represents the most perfect act of obedience which it is given to man to accomplish. It follows that all other human activities, command over men, technical planning, art, science, philosophy and so on, are all inferior to physical labour in spiritual significance. It is not difficult to define the place that physical labour should occupy in a well ordered social life. It should be its core" (1952:288). One's attitude to labour, like one's attitude to death, defines one's attitude to life: whether one seeks self-affirmation by means of self-assertion or by self-donation.

Work and money

The two aspects of human persons, the personal and the impersonal, are also reflected in the sphere of work in the relationship between work and money. In terms of these two aspects, money has two meanings in its relationship to work: capital and ownership.

By capital I refer to the totality of the resources for work or means of production, including nature itself as transformed by centuries of labour into materials and instruments and a variety of infrastructures for the work process. It is important to understand capital in this way because such an insight enables one to see capital as the result of work, and hence in a position of subordination and service vis-a-vis the actual work process, and even more so in relation to the workers themselves.

John Paul II makes this point when he asserts that "Since the concept of capital includes not only the natural resources placed at man's disposal but also the whole collection of means by which man appropriates natural resources and transforms them in accordance with his needs ... it must immediately be noted that all these means are the result of the historical heritage of human labour" (1981:30). From this there follows what he refers to as "the principle of the priority of labour over capital" (1981:28). Capital is related to work as its instrument. Hence there is no necessary opposition between them. The one is meant to serve the other, and both to serve the workers themselves.

Ownership is the other aspect of the function of money in the sphere of work. As with capital, ownership must be seen in relation to work and, especially, to the person of the worker. Ownership of the means of production – whether private or public – derives from the nature of work itself. Unless access to instruments and materials is assured to the workers, the work cannot go forward, and the natural desires of the workers will be frustrated, and the common good will not be served. Thus ownership of the means of production derives from the necessity of work in human life, and must always serve work and its importance in human life. The right to private property (or private capital) is thus subordinate to the right to the common use of the means of production in ways that serve the common good. Collective ownership, on the other hand, is only legitimate when it serves the purpose of enabling individual workers to grow as persons in co-operative and creative work. Uncontrolled capitalism or absolute socialism without any restraints can thus never be economic systems that meet our criteria of personal growth and community.

Criteria for liberation in the sphere of work

Our philosophy of persons has provided us with a particular understanding of the nature and importance of work in human life. We must now try and see what light it can throw on the human predicament insofar as it shows itself in the world of work.

Human persons are both personal and bodily beings, self-realising and other-dependent. In the sphere of work this shows itself in a twofold relatedness: to other persons in the very process of work, and to the impersonal world that provides the material and instruments of our work. Thus there will be a twofold criterion for liberation in the sphere of work, two indications of whether or not the practices and institutions and methods of work foster or impede the personal growth and community that is appropriate in this sphere of life.

The first is solidarity. And it has many aspects: co-operation between workers in the work process, common ownership of the means of production, communication between workers of different kinds, the connection between training for work and general education, the connection between working life and family life, are some of the most important. Solidarity is the criterion of personal growth in relation to other persons in the sphere of work.

The second criterion is creativity. This is the criterion of personal growth in one's relation to the impersonal aspect of work, its techniques and training, the technology itself, the materials and products, productivity and profits. Creativity connotes productivity of what is genuinely valuable, as well as the human value of the productive activity itself, an activity in which the meaning we give to our lives is embodied and symbolised. Creativity also entails other human values such as freedom and entertainment, the notion that work should be a pleasure as well as useful.

These two criteria for liberation in the sphere of work will determine the actual ways we will try to change this sphere of our lives. But they also can help us to see the way in which the actual working world falls short of being a means and an expression of personal growth and community, and constitutes instead a predicament from which we need to be freed.

The human predicament in the world of work

The classical modern account of the human predicament in the sphere of work is Marx's theory of alienation. This is so well-known and so much has been written on it, that I will outline it only briefly here, with a view to bringing out the parallels between it and our own account of the basic structure of the human predicament.

The idea of alienation has its philosophical roots in the work of Hegel, being an essential aspect of the Hegelian view of human nature we noted in Chapter Six. According to this view human life, whether of the individual or the group, is a process of the subject objectifying or externalising themselves in some or other activity, and then reappropriating or identifying with this resulting objective state of affairs, so as both to make it really part of their own personal life, and to realise themselves as its originator.

Marx inherits the essentials of this view of human nature from Hegel but applies it especially in the sphere of work. By work we externalise our subjective ideas and values in the world of nature, thereby "humanising" nature in the products of our labour or, as Marx would put it, creating a "human nature". Marx understands this latter expression in a very literal way. The product of human labour is the first and only genuine human nature; the biological antecedents of labour being human only in a secondary and philosophically uninteresting way. Because of this, the externalised product of our labour, understood comprehensively as all that has been produced in the course of human history, social forms and cultural objects as well as tools and the means of life, assumes an immense importance. It is, quite simply, our objective humanity. We are only human to the extent that we are able to identify with it, appropriate it, engage with it in our lives. Hence to be separated from it in any way amounts to the loss of all that is precious in human life, all that makes life worth living. Separation of this kind is what is meant by alienation.

Marx's theory of alienation

Marx's theory of alienation was developed in a particular context, that of nineteenth-century capitalist industrialisation, but applies *mutatis mutandis* to any work situation that shares the characteristics of that context. And this includes virtually all of the industrially developed parts of the world, and much of the undeveloped parts as well.

According to Marx, alienation in the sphere of work comprises four elements. The worker becomes alienated from the product of their work, from the work process itself, from what Marx calls their "species being", and from other people. Briefly these different aspects of alienation can be described as follows:

Workers are alienated from the product of their labour because they do not own it; it belongs to the owner of the means of production, the capital. Where the product is seen in the comprehensive way described above, this lack of ownership has far reaching consequences. Workers can find themselves excluded from all the goods and services made available by their labour. The means of access to these is money, and the economic system ensures that they never have enough.

Workers are alienated from the work process because it is a means to an end, not an end in itself. Work is an activity with a goal that is extrinsic to it, money, rather than one that is a fulfilment of the activity itself. People work in order to live, rather than (as Marx would have it) live in order to work – in the sense of expressing their creativity. Work of this kind, since it is not the expression of a creative desire, but only a means to satisfy an animal need, has a dehumanising effect on people that shows in the mindless and sometimes brutal forms of leisure activity it generates. Life alternates between the forced activity of work and the drugged passivity of leisure. Furthermore the nature of the work is determined by the nature of the product rather than the person of the worker, and this can reinforce its dehumanising effect.

Workers are alienated from their "species being". This is the deepest, most interior aspect of alienation. It is the loss of a sense of one's humanity, not as an abstract or theoretical truth, but as the sense of oneself as a free, self-determining origin of thought and action and as a co-creator of culture and society.

Finally workers are alienated from other people. This aspect of alienation shows itself most clearly in the separation and estrangement between workers and owners as distinct classes. But their is also the opposition of competition for money between each worker and the others, and between each owner and the rest. The system of labour reduces all intercourse betweeen persons to the level of money. A person's value is determined by the money they either earn or own. Work itself, and the worker too, are regarded as commodities that can be bought and sold.

Such is the picture of the human predicament in the sphere of work provided by Marx's theory of alienation. And certainly the world of work appears in it as one devoid of solidarity and creativity. To this extent the predicament has the character that our philosophy of persons would lead one to expect. But it is when we consider the account given of the *causes* of alienation that the similarity is most marked. Division of labour and private property are fundamental elements in the system of alienated labour but they are not its ultimate cause. The ultimate cause of alienation is the idolatrous attitude to money.

Marx speaks of the "divine power of money" (Fromm, 1961:166) and explains this as it having the character of "the alienated and self-alienating species-life of man. It is the alienated power of humanity" (Fromm, 1961:166). Humanity has externalised and objectified its own powers in the external object of money, which is now seen as the source of all that is valuable in life. The desire for money is the desire for total control over one's life, and this of course includes control over all the factors on which one's life depends, other people and the impersonal world as well.

It is this idol-creating desire that is the true source and energy of alienation. Tucker gives a vivid description of how Marx saw it: "a kind of acquisitive mania that sees in money the means of exercising power over everything. Man worships money as the 'externalised potentiality of mankind' and 'almighty being' that confers unlimited power upon its possessor ... This all-embracing passion ... is seen by Marx as an 'utterly alien power' or 'inhuman force' that holds sway over the whole of human existence. It has been the motive force of the historical process up to now. Man has created his objective world under its iron compulsion. Marx calls it 'alien' and 'inhuman' because he sees in it the force that alienates man from himself, deprives him of freedom and dehumanises him" (Tucker, 1967:138–139). Marx brings out very powerfully the unlimited and absolutising character of this passion and the way in which it annihilates all other human interests and desires. It amounts to humanity's self-destruction of its own humanity.

Materialism: theoretical and practical

As one would expect Simone Weil echoes Marx's insight into the dehumanising power of work. Because of the centrality of work in human life, if society is built on a mistaken conception of work, one is bound to put an idol of some kind in the place left in one's heart by the absence of an authentic devotion to one's work. A civilisation "founded on the spiritual nature of work" is the "only thing great enough to put before the peoples instead of the totalitarian idol." (She is thinking of both the fascist and the communist systems.) "If it is not put before them in such a way as to make them feel its grandeur, they will remain in the grip of the idol; only it will be painted red instead of brown" (1952:92).

The theoretical and practical materialism underlying both capitalism and communism always contain the potential of undermining the subjectivity of the workers and representing and treating them not as persons but as things. John Paul II emphasises this when he writes that "the danger of treating work as a special kind of 'merchandise', or as an impersonal 'force' needed for production (the expression 'work force' is, in fact, in common use) always exists, especially when the whole way of looking at the question of economics is marked by the premises of materialistic economism" (1981:18).

In capitalism the worker is treated "on the same level as the whole complex of the material means of production, as an instrument and not in accordance with the true dignity of his work – that is to say, where he is not treated as subject and maker, and for this very reason as the true purpose of the whole process of production" (1981:19). In communism too the humanity of the worker is lost sight of: "In dialectical materialism too man is not first and foremost the subject of work and the efficient cause of the production process, but continues to be understood and treated, in dependence on what is material, as a kind of resultant of the economic or production relations prevailing at a given period" (1981:33).

In *Small is Beautiful* Schumacher blames materialism, both as a theory of human nature and as system of values, for the progressive dehumanisation of the world of work in the twentieth century. In addition to its inability to understand human beings as subjects and persons, it affects the way we see and use the instruments and materials of work and nature itself. No restraints are placed on our development and use of technological power, nor on our use of natural sources of energy. In the pursuit of the goals of production the environment is poisoned and people are actually impoverished. A world of scarcity is created. Above all a materialistic philosophy of life sanctions and even encourages what Gandhi criticised: "dreaming of systems so perfect that no-one will need to be good" (Schumacher 1973:18)

But it is not only the attitude to work that dehumanises the worker. The way work is organised, and the conditions of work in a modern industrialised society, are equally dehumanising. Weil gives a graphic account of the effect becoming a worker can have on a person: "First of all we must do away with the shock experienced by a lad who at twelve or thirteen leaves school and enters a factory. There are some workmen who could feel happy enough, had this shock not left behind it an ever-open wound; but they don't realise themselves that their suffering comes to them from the past. The child while at school, whether a good or bad pupil, was a being whose existence was recognised, whose development was a matter of concern, whose best motives were appealed to. From one day to the next, he finds himself an extra cog in a machine, rather less than a thing, and nobody cares any more whether he obeys from the lowest motives or not, provided he obeys. The majority of workmen have at anyrate at this stage of their lives experienced the sensation of no longer existing, accompanied by a sort of inner vertigo, such as intellectuals or bourgeois, even in their greatest sufferings, have very rarely had the opportunity of knowing. This first shock, received at so early an age, often leaves an indelible mark. It can rule out all love of work once and for all" (1952:51).

Finally it must be said that it is not only the mechanistic way in which work is organised, and the mechanisation of the work process, that dehumanises the workers, but the actual machinery that they have to use. This will be apparent in our account of liberation in the sphere of work that follows.

The liberation of work: solidarity

As we have said the liberation process that enables the achievement of personal growth and community in the sphere of work must meet the demands of the two principles of solidarity and creativity.

The principle of solidarity will manifest itself in three particular forms: subsidiarity, integration and new forms of ownership.

Subsidiarity

The notion of subsidiarity is central to the European humanist tradition, though now honoured more in the breach than in the observance. Here is a celebrated formulation of it: "It is an injustice, and at the same time a grave evil and disturbance of right order to assign to a greater and higher association what lesser and subordinate associations can do. For every social activity ought of its very nature to furnish help to the members of the body social and never destroy and absorb them. Those in command should be sure that the more perfectly a graduated order is preserved among the various associations, in observing the principle of subsidiary function, the stronger will be the social authority and effectiveness and the happier and more prosperous the condition of the State" (Pius XI, 1931).

The central idea here is that in any association, whether we are thinking of the organisation of work or of society as a whole, the centre exists for the circumference, the whole for the part. And this is because any association is made up of persons, and must exist for the sake of the persons who comprise it. Schumacher gives an amusing image of this principle as applied to the sphere of work: a man holding a bunch of balloons. He actually applies the image to a project he carried out for the National Coal Board of Great Britain, in which he dispersed the huge conglomerate into seventeen "quasi-firms", each serving a distinct function and with its own autonomy for that purpose. They continued to be linked, however, to a central administration which existed simply for the purpose of enabling each to fulfil its function, by integrating the output of all the different firms.

The notion of subsidiarity can be applied to a whole economy as well as to a single business. This is especially important in the case of the undeveloped countries of the world where the problem of poverty is, as Schumacher puts it, "the problem of two million villages" (1973:162). What is needed for the real liberation of the workers of the world is not more centralisation of massive, hi-tech, capital intensive industries, but two million new work-places, organised around medium-sized regional centres which will supply what they need but cannot themselves produce.

The principle of subsidiarity is not opposed to centralisation as such. In fact in our present predicament it could be used to argue for more world-wide centralisation than exists at present. Surely the distribution of essential foodstuffs, strategic materials and medicines ought to be centralised on a global scale. There probably ought to be a centralisation of military power as well in the form of some world-wide peace-keeping or police force. (And thus an end to private armies – by which I mean such armies as those of South Africa and the United States). The absolute autonomy of our modern nation-states seems a thoroughly irrational arrangement, and a continuing threat to world-wide peace and prosperity. It is by no means a natural example of subsidiarity. In terms of that principle the developed nations exist, as far as economic matters are concerned, for the sake of the undeveloped ones. They are to produce those things needed by the world economy which can only be produced in huge technologically sophisticated plants. The aid they can give to the rest of the world in this respect is not an option but a necessity.

Integration

The idea of integration is another element in the principle of solidarity in the world of work. It must be referred both to different spheres in the life of the individual and to different kinds of work and worker.

In the first place there must be integration between the family-life and the working life of the worker, and between home and school. Places of work, factories for instance, should be de-centralised so as to avoid separation between working life and home life. Weil has a beautiful description of an economic order which observes this principle of integration which I cannot resist quoting at length: "Some men could work at home; others in small workshops, which could very often be organized on a co-operative basis ...

Such workshops would not be small factories, they would be industrial organisms of a new kind, in which a new spirit could blow; though small, they would be bound together by organic ties strong enough to enable them to form as a whole a large concern. There is about large concerns, in spite of all their defects, a special sort of poetry, and one for which workmen have nowadays acquired a taste ... Whether on a co-operative basis or not, these little workshops would at any rate not be like prisons. A workman would be able now and again to show his wife where he works and his machine ... The children would come along, after school, to join their father and learn how to work, at an age when work is by far the most exciting of all games. Thus, later on, when they came to start their apprenticeship, they would already be almost qualified in one trade ... Work would be lit up by poetry for the rest of their lives by these wonders experienced in infancy, instead of wearing throughout life the gloomy aspect of a nightmare, simply because of the shock received on initiation" (1952:57–58).

Training of workers of all kinds should be de-centralised in a similar way to workshops, and based on an apprenticeship model. It should be interspersed with academic education so that vocational training and a broader academic education are not separated, even in idea, from each other. As Weil says, "The popular school's job is to give more dignity to work by infusing it with thought, and not to make of the working-man a thing divided up into compartments which sometimes works and sometimes thinks" (1952:90).

Modern means of production create a divide between industrial and agricultural workers. This division needs to be overcome, especially since workers in the countryside always tend to think that the workers in the towns are better off, the towns being the principal centres of growth. For this reason it is important that agricultural workers should own their own property, which should be regarded as raw material for carrying on work. It is also important, in terms of the principle of integration, that young industrial and agricultural workers should mix with intellectuals and middle-class youth during the period of their education. Unions and civic and religious organisations are favourable milieus for such mixing to occur.

New forms of ownership

The principle of solidarity in the world of work also suggests the need for new forms of ownership of the means of production. The interdependence between private enterprise and the public infrastructure that supports it, is an inevitable fact of economic life, and should be recognised in reciprocal financial responsibility between the private and the public sector of society.

As far as ownership is concerned, our philosophy of persons would indicate arrangements where individual and group are not in opposition to each other, where individual freedom and responsibility to the community are reconciled. An attempt should be made to combine the "capitalist" with the "socialist" virtues in each business or economy. This is not the place to discuss ways in which this could be done, even if I were able. Schumacher suggests several in *Small is Beautiful,* one at least of which has actually been tried, has succeeded, and endures and still flourishes, some forty years after it started. The Scott-Bader Commonwealth is such a symbol of how solidarity in ownership in the world of work may be achieved, that I will outline the bare essentials of the scheme here, in the hope that it may inspire the reader to find out more about it.

Scott-Bader was a plastics company started by Ernest Bader in 1920. By 1951 it was a flourishing medium-sized business. Acting out of a desire to create a business whose primary function was to serve the good of the workers, Mr. Bader then proceeded to transfer ownership of the company into the hands of the Commonwealth, of which every single person who worked in the company was an equal member.

The Commonwealth had some simple rules. Firstly, it was to be of limited size (350 persons) "so that every person in it can embrace it in his mind and imagination" (1973:231). Secondly, wages were not to vary, between the lowest and highest paid, beyond a range of 1:7. Thirdly, as co-owners no-one could be dismissed except for gross personal misconduct. Fourthly, 60% of the profits were to be retained for taxation and for self-finance within the company. The remaining 40% was to be used equally for the payment of bonuses to all workers and for charitable purposes outside the organisation. Finally, none of the products were to be sold to customers who would use them for war-related purposes.

On this basis the Company was constituted and still exists today. It does just as well as other companies, and better than most. Moreover its example has led to the foundation of close on 1700 similar worker-owned companies in Great Britain alone. Its profitability shows the possibility of organising the sphere of work in a way that does justice to the true nature of the freedom of persons, namely the interdependence of individual and social freedom. In particular the Scott-Bader experiment illustrates some important conditions for humanising the world of work.

The transfer of ownership from an individual to a collectivity changes the existential character of ownership for every person involved. In fact ownership in the traditional sense has been replaced by specific rights and responsibilities in the administration of common assets. There is no gap between individual and common good.

The whole enterprise grew from the personal sacrifice of one man, who abandoned voluntarily the chance of becoming inordinately rich and powerful. Excessive wealth is necessarily alienating for an individual; too great a disparity of wealth makes personal community impossible.

The tasks of a business organisation within society are not simply to make profits. That is one. There is also a technical task, that of improving product design the better to satisfy the need to which it caters. There is a social task, namely that of providing members of the company with opportunities for satisfaction and development through their participation in the working community. Finally there is a political task: to encourage people by example to work towards a more humane economic order. Scott-Bader, as it presently exists, takes this last task very seriously. I have personal knowledge of their commitment to and involvement in the struggle for liberation in the world of work in the new South Africa.

The liberation of work: creativity

We come finally to the principle of creativity in the sphere of work, and a brief consideration of its implications. There are three notions which I find helpful here: those of technology "with a human face", intermediate technology and appropriate aid. They can be simply explained.

Here, as elsewhere in this chapter, I am chiefly indebted to Schumacher for the concrete application of ethical ideas to economic realities. The expression "technology with a human face" is his (1973:128). In general it refers to machinery made with the worker rather than the product primarily in mind. This must be cheap enough so that it is accessible to virtually everyone, suitable for small-scale application and compatible with our need for creativity. It is not difficult to see that such machinery is well-adapted to the requirements of subsidiarity and integration as outlined above. In particular it is compatible with the idea of "intermediate technology", namely technology that is appropriate for use in the majority of the countries of the world, which are still largely undeveloped.

Gandhi preached production by the masses rather than mass production. In the spirit of this Schumacher writes, "The system of mass production, based on sophisticated, highly capital-intensive, high energy-input dependent, and human labour-saving technology, presupposes that you are already rich, for a great deal of capital investment is needed to establish one single workplace. The system of production by the masses mobilises the priceless resources which are possessed by all human beings, their clever brains and skilful hands, and supports them with first-class tools. The technology of mass production is inherently violent, ecologically damaging, self-defeating in terms of non-renewable resources, and stultifying for the human person. The technology of production by the masses, making use of the best of modern knowledge and experience, is conducive to de-centralisation, compatible with the laws of ecology, gentle in its use of scarce resources, and designed to serve the human person instead of making him the servant of machines. I have named it *intermediate technology* to signify that it is vastly superior to the primitive technology of bygone ages but at the same time much simpler, cheaper and freer than the super-technology of the rich. One can also call it self-help technology, or democratic or people's technology – a technology to which everybody can gain admittance and which is not reserved to those already rich and powerful" (1973:128). If only the leaders of Third World countries would heed the wisdom of this powerful passage!

Creativity in the world of work applies also to the development and organisation of new work-places. This is what I refer to as "appropriate aid". "Aid" has become a notorious name for the influence a First World power can exert on a Third World one. But there is no reason why aid need be dependence-creating and exploitative. Within the framework of subsidiarity sketched above, the best aid a First World country can give a Third World one is useful knowledge, knowledge of how to produce, to organise and use the technology appropriate to their situation and their needs.

The subject of knowledge brings me to the end of our study of liberation in the sphere of work. In the last resort liberation in this sphere – and indeed in any other – must be the activity of those who stand in need of it. They can have guides certainly, but the actual liberation must be something done by them and in them. And whatever else it involves, it must involve a change in consciousness, consciousness of themselves and their power. In other words an access of self-knowledge. Both Weil and Schumacher see education as the soul of liberation, especially in the sphere of work.

It is not however technical education that they regard as fundamental. Each in their own way pleads for a kind of general education that will counter the popular contemporary myths that control people's minds and make for an inhuman world (Schumacher) or change our false conceptions of goodness and human flourishing (Weil). Each ends up by asserting the need for a world-view and system of values that can only be called philosophical. For the moment let us let the matter rest there. But with a further question: Is philosophy enough? Education is a necessary condition to be sure, but is it a sufficient one?

Chapter Twelve

Gender: Equality and Complementarity

Let us now consider the sphere of gender in human life and how our understanding of the necessary conditions of personal growth and community can guide the struggle for liberation in this sphere.

As in the case of work, almost everything I shall have to say concerning liberation in the sphere of gender will be controversial, both in an academic and in a broadly political sense. I have not the space, and possibly not the ability, to engage profitably in these controversies here and now. I do however feel I ought to remind the reader that I am trying to see what guidance philosophy – and in particular the philosophy of persons we have developed in this book – can give us in understanding and overcoming the predicament we face in the different concrete spheres of life. Science, and especially the human sciences, can greatly increase our understanding of these spheres of life, and also provide us with ways and means of achieving liberation there. But they cannot provide us with the fundamental concepts that illuminate the predicament as one involving persons, and the values that indicate the nature of the liberation that we need. For that we need philosophy.

In the sphere of gender, as I hope to show, the achievement of personal growth and community on the one hand, and the development and expression of gender identity on the other, are so bound up with each other that it is difficult and unwieldy to separate the one from the other. And I shall not do so. This means that my account of the different stages of our development and enactment of our gendered life will be a normative and ideal account, and to that extent an abstract one – though less so than my acccount of the necessary conditions for personal growth. It should not for that reason be dismissed as fanciful. It is intended to tell the truth about how gendered persons can best be enabled to develop as persons. Nevertheless, for example, when I deal with a child's relationship with the nursing mother, I will assume that the mother is the child's natural mother, that she is not a single parent, cruel, insane and so on.

In the sphere of gender even the language one uses to define one's subject matter is controversial, so I shall make my own position clear at the outset. I shall use the term "gender" to designate everything that distinguishes women from men, the physical and biological as well as the psychic and mental. I do this because I am not a philosophical dualist and so do not accept the fiction of men and women having spiritually identical minds in physically different bodies. Nor am I a materialist and so do not think of men and women simply as physical bodies, and so different in every way. Human persons have an irreducible unity of life and it is essentially and differentially gendered. So I use the term "gender" to refer to what makes women different from men. "Sex" and "sexual" I use only to refer to the erotic dimension of life.

The nature of gender

In order to situate our study of liberation in the sphere of gender in a genuinely philosophical context, I am going to tell two stories.

In Plato's *Symposium* the guests at the banquet each makes a speech in honour of love. Aristophanes, the poet, tells a comic tale about the origin of sex, as his contribution to the conversation.

In the beginning, he says, we humans were spherical creatures, equipped with double of everything we have today, four legs, four arms, two faces turned in opposite directions and so on, genitals included. We were very full of ourselves, full of pride, so much so that we disputed the possession of heaven with the gods. The gods were worried by us and decided to punish and weaken us by dividing us in two "like eggs which are cut with a hair". Since then the separated halves have searched for each other, longing to be whole again. And when, as happens, we find our other half we throw our arms about each other and refuse ever to be separated again, bound together by the passion which we call love. If, Aristophanes suggests, one of the gods were to ask two lovers what they hoped to gain from each other, and expressed his question in this way: "Is the object of your desire to be always together as much as possible, and never to be separated from one another day or night? If that is what you want, I am ready to melt and weld you together, so that, instead of two, you shall be one flesh; as long as you live you shall live a common life, and when you die, you shall suffer a common death, and be still one, not two, even in the next world. Would such a fate as this content you, and satisfy your longing?" there could be no doubt that everyone would answer *Yes*." And so Aristophanes concludes his story with his definition that love (and he is talking of sexual love) is "simply the name for the desire and pursuit of the whole" (1951:59–65).

There is another story, from another tradition, with which most of us are more familiar but – for that reason – have probably not really reflected on, that makes a similar point. It goes as follows:

"The Lord God said, 'It is not good that the man should be alone. I will make him a helpmate.' So from the soil the Lord God fashioned all the wild beasts and all the birds of heaven. Those he brought to the man to see what he would call them; each one was to bear the name the man would give it. The man gave names to all the cattle, all the birds of heaven and all the wild beasts. But no helpmate suitable for man was found for him. So the Lord God made the man fall into a deep sleep. And while he slept, he took one of his ribs and enclosed it in flesh. The Lord God built the rib he had taken from the man into a woman, and brought her to the man. The man exclaimed: 'This at last is bone from my bone, and flesh from my flesh! This is to be called woman, for this was taken from man.' This is why a man leaves his father and mother and joins himself to his wife, and they become one body" (Genesis 2,18–24).

This story, like that of Aristophanes', explains sexual desire as the desire for union with another because of our individual incompleteness so that together we might form a unified whole. By nature we desire to be part of a whole in which the other makes up something we lack, complements and so completes us. But Genesis goes further than Aristophanes; it links this desire to the fact of gender. If we take sexual love between a man and a woman as the typical case, as the story in Genesis does, then it is clear that each has something that the other has not but which is essential for the creation of the whole, the one body of humanity. Each lacks what the other has and so each is complementary for the other. Together they constitute a single whole that contains and expresses all of human nature. Only within that whole is each able to realise to the full their own nature as a male or female human being.

The book of Genesis is quite emphatic that it is only when men and women are taken together, as complementing and completing one another in a natural unity or whole, that they constitute the "image of God" that humanity is. This is how I understand the first creation story in the book of Genesis. It has God saying "Let us make man in our image, after our likeness", and then, "So God created man in his own image, in the image of God he created him; male and female he created them"(Genesis1,1–2,4). "Man" here means human beings, humankind or humanity. And it is affirming that it is part of human nature to be gendered and differently so. The gender difference is an essential part of the humanity that is the image of God.

The philosophical truth expressed in these two stories, taken from the twin roots of the European philosophical tradition, is more or less that which I have been at pains to labour in this book: that human persons depend on other persons for the exercise, development and fulfilment of their humanity, or as the African tradition would have it, *umuntu ngumuntu ngabantu.* In these stories however this truth is situated in the dimension of gender. Here gender expresses the fact that otherness – and so difference – is a feature of the very human nature of human (which is to say bodily) persons. The fulness of human nature is not realised in any single human individual but only in the male and female couple. This difference "within" the nature of human persons is the basis for the idea of the complementarity of genders which is given such powerful and amusing expression in these stories.

Human persons are equally persons but complementary in their gendered humanity. Consequently personal growth and community in the sphere of gender must be characterised by equality and complementarity. These then will be the principles of liberation (corresponding to those of solidarity and creativity in the sphere of work) in this sphere of human life.

The development of gender

In discussing the development of gender identity and expression in relation to our growth as persons, I will have of necessity to deal with material that is proper to the sciences. I am not competent to authenticate it; in a summary such as this all I can do is refer the reader to my sources.

This is not the place to give a detailed account of the differences in bodily structure and functioning in the different genders. But, since in a non-dualistic account of human persons such as ours, bodily differences will entail psychic and mental differences as well, I must say something about these, however brief.

In the generation of a human being the products of the male and female bodies play equal and complementary roles. Both genders provide what only they can give. Each moreover, the sperm and the ovule, has to lose half of its nuclear potential in order to combine in the act of fertilisation. The product of the act, the new human being, is a synthesis of elements that only different genders can provide.

Forty-six chromosomes make up the human gene, half from each parent, forming 23 functional pairs. One pair determines gender; to it the mother always contributes the same kind of chromosome (called X after its shape), but the father's contribution varies, being either the same X kind or a different kind called Y (for the same reason). If it is X the baby will be a girl, if Y a boy.

In the sixth week of foetal life the male gene produces testosterone, a hormone that causes the developing sexual organs of the baby to assume a male form. This doesn't happen in the case of the female gene, and the baby continues its developement as female.

At the same time as determining the structure of the body and its sexual organs, this hormonal activity determines the structure of the brain, which is different and differently organised in males and females.

The only general physical diffference in structure between the brains of men and women is in the *corpus callosum*, the bundle of fibres that connects the two hemispheres. The core of this connection, which enables the two hemispheres to share and integrate their functioning, is significantly larger in women than in men.

In addition to this purely physical difference, there are a number of differences in the spatial location of different brain functions (such as the mechanics of language, vocabulary and verbal definition, visuo-spatial perception, emotion) in men and women, and differences too in the specificity or diffuseness of such localisation. These differences underlie gender-specific tendencies to differences in aptitude and ability of various kinds (Moir and Jessel, 1989; Oraison, 1967).

Such natural tendencies to differences in aptitude and ability are reinforced in the interpersonal transaction between the baby and the nursing mother after birth. Since conception the mother has been the total and totally sufficient environment for the baby, the sole source of satisfaction for both its bodily and strictly personal needs. After birth, in spite of the trauma of separation from the womb, the baby does not differentiate between itself and the mother; there is a symbiotic identity between mother and child. The mother, however, from the first moment after birth, responds to the baby as a distinct person and as either a boy or a girl, the same gender as she is or different. This recognition by the mother is (as our philosophy of persons would lead us to expect) the original source of the child's own awareness of its gender.

The fundamental asymmetry in respect of gender in the nursing relationship is reinforced as the child grows up. For both girl and boy the mother is identified with the self. And growth for the girl is becoming more like her mother. In personal growth both boy and girl must move from self (mother) to other (father), but the movement is not symmetrical, the girl identifying herself with her mother (herself), the boy with his father (the other). One can say that the boy has further to go to find himself. He has to assimilate the other, the girl simply has to reinforce the self-identification with the mother. Thus the self-consciousness that is constitutive of personhood has a different modality for each gender, a modality that is all-pervasive of a person's life and foundational to all their subsequent experience (Oraison, 1967; Mead, 1950).

Gender identity is fully established by this process of identification and complementation with those of the same and the opposite gender by the time the child is three or four. It parallels almost exactly the acquisition of language. There is no new hormonal activity during this period. And once established, gender identity is irreversible, no matter what operations may be performed or hormones administered.

During the whole period of childhood, gender differences become more consciously experienced and are heightened as a consequence. The process reaches a climax in puberty when different hormones in each gender bring the bodies of both to sexual maturity. Adolescence is also the climax of the interpersonal transaction with the parents in which the child experiences its gender identity. The girl has to define herself in relation to her father, overcoming the rivalry with her mother in the process; the boy has to define himself in relation to his mother overcoming the rivalry with his father. In this way each prepares for full sexual encounter with the opposite gender. As at the beginning of their discovery of their gender identity so too at its climax in puberty, the asymmetry of male and female experience is apparent.

The girl's initial sense of incompleteness at lacking external sex organs is superseded by her awareness of having everything that is needed to be a woman, to be a mother and bear a child. She is now truly like her mother; the process of her development has come full circle back to its beginning. From now on her gender identity is focussed on what is internal to her, her womb and its capacity to hold life and produce it. This gives a distinctive character to her whole emotional life and to her experience of sex.

The boy, on the other hand, had a period of initial pride, but now experiences incompleteness in the face of the prospect of becoming a man like his father and producing a child. He has the power to be sure, but he can never be certain that he will succeed and that the child will be his, his possession, in the way it clearly is mother's. His gender identity is focussed on an external sexual organ and what he must find and penetrate in order to become a father. This difference of focus gives its own distinctive character to his emotional life and sexual experience too (Mead, 1950).

Gender identity and personal growth

What follows in this section are, of course, the results of scientific studies. I have no way of establishing their validity. They are thus presented not as "proofs" of a particular philosophical point of view, but as illustrations of it. As such they possess their own suggestive force.

Throughout the development of gender identity up to and including adolescence, there is also taking place (or not, as the case may be) personal growth in the strict sense in which we have defined it in our philosophy of persons. Both take place in relation to a variety of significant others, initially the parents but increasingly peer groups of the same and opposite gender. We have sketched the differences in the development of gender identity in men and women. I want now to say something about how gender difference affects (as we should expect it to) the character of personal growth itself in the different genders.

Gender differences are seen in the differences for men and women in the patterns of moral experience and understanding. According to Carol Gilligan (1983), for men the index of personal growth is the development of autonomy, through the separation of the individual from the original bond attachment to the mother; the moral challenge is that of coming to see others as of equal value to oneself. For women personal growth is seen as the development of relationships. The original attachment is reinforced so that it moves towards the interdependence of love and care. The moral issue is that of self-affirmation within this network of relations. Men have difficulty in getting emotionally connected with others; women have difficulty in seeing themselves as good.

Different genders have different attitudes to aggression: men see violence in closeness and fear domination, women see it in apartness and fear self-assertion. Men see danger in being trapped and failing to achieve; women see danger in being set apart by success. The task for the man is to limit aggression, for the woman to sustain connection (Gilligan,1983).

Men and women also have different natural fantasy patterns, designated by Robert May as "Pride" and "Caring".

"The 'male pattern' of fantasy that Robert May (1980) identifies as 'Pride' in his studies of sex differences in projective imagination leads from enhancment to deprivation and continues the story that Freud has told of an initial fracture of connection leading through the experience of separation to an irreparable loss, a glorious achievement followed by a disastrous fall. But the pattern of female fantasy May designates as 'Caring' traces a path which remains largely unexplored, a narrative of deprivation followed by enhancment in which connection, though leading through separation, is in the end maintained or restored. Illuminating life as a web rather than a succession of relationships, women portray autonomy rather than attachment as the illusory and dangerous quest. In this way women's development points towards a different history of human attachment, stressing continuity and change in configuration, rather than replacement and separation, elucidating a different response to loss, and changing the metaphor of growth" (Gilligan, 1983:48).

There are also different images of the relation of the self with others which relate to differences of gender. These are those of "hierarchy" and "web".

"While the truths of psychological theory have blinded psychologists to the truth of women's experience, that experience illuminates a world which psychologists have found hard to trace, a territory where violence is rare and relationships appear safe. The reason women's experience has been so difficult to decipher or even discern is that a shift in the imagery of relationships gives rise to a problem of interpretation. The images of hierarchy and web, drawn from the text's of men's and women's fantasies and thoughts, convey different ways of structuring relationships and are associated with different views of morality and self. But these images create a problem in understanding because each distorts the other's representation. As the top of the hierarchy becomes the edge of the web and as the centre of a network of connection becomes the middle of a hierarchical progression, each image marks as dangerous the place which the other defines as safe.

Thus the images of hierarchy and web inform different modes of assertion and response: the wish to be alone at the top and the consequent fear that others will get too close; the wish to be at the centre of connection and the consequent fear of being too far out on the edge. These disparate fears of being stranded and being caught give rise to different portrayals of achievement and affiliation, leading to different modes of action and different ways of assessing the consequences of choice" (Gilligan, 1983:62).

These differences in fundamental imagery determine differences in approach to morality. Where men emphasise rights, women emphasise responsibility. Whereas men seek impartial judgment on the basis of equality through the agreement of all rational people, women seek to respond with selective care to each different situation of need. Men stress the justice of non-interference, women the necessity of caring involvement.

"The moral imperative that emerges repeatedly in interviews with women is an injunction to care, a responsibility to discern and alleviate the 'real and recognisable trouble' of this world. For men, the moral imperative appears rather as an injunction to respect the rights of others and thus to protect from interference the rights to life and self-fulfilment. Women's insistence on care is at first self-critical rather than self-protective, while men initially conceive obligation to others negatively in terms of non-interference. Development for both sexes would therefore seem to entail an integration of rights and responsibilities through the discovery of the complementarity of these disparate views. For women, the integration of rights and responsibilities takes place through an understanding of the psychological logic of relationships. This understanding tempers the self-destructive potential of a self-critical morality by asserting the need of all persons for care. For men, recognition through experience of the need for more active responsibility in taking care corrects the potential indifference of a morality of non-interference and turns attention from the logic to the consequences of choice" (Gilligan and Murphy, 1979; Gilligan, 1981). "In the development of a post-conventional ethical understanding, women come to see the violence inherent in inequality, while men come to see the limitations of a conception of justice blinded to the differences in human life" (Gilligan, 1983:100).

Thus the personal growth of men and women generates different but complementary moral insights. "In the transition from adolescence to adulthood, the dilemma itself is the same for both sexes, a conflict between integrity and care. But approached from different perspectives, this dilemma generates the recognition of opposite truths. These different perspectives are reflected in two different moral ideologies, since separation is justified by an ethic of rights while attachment is supported by an ethic of care.

The morality of rights is predicated on equality and centred on the understanding of fairness, while the ethic of responsibility relies on the concept of equity, the recognition of differences in need. While the ethic of rights is a manifestation of equal respect, balancing the claims of other and self, the ethic of responsibility rests on an understanding that gives rise to compassion and care. Thus the counterpoint of identity and intimacy that marks the time between childhood and adulthood is articulated through two different moralities whose complementarity is the discovery of maturity" (Gilligan 1983:164).

Moral maturity consists in coming to combine these insights into morality by being able to see the world through the eyes of the other gender.

"To understand how the tension between responsibilities and rights sustains the dialectic of human development is to see the integrity of two disparate modes of experience that are in the end connected. While an ethic of justice proceeds from the premise of equality – that everyone should be treated the same – an ethic of care rests on the premise of non-violence – that no-one should be hurt. In the representation of maturity, both perspectives converge in the realisation that just as inequality adversely affects both parties in an unequal relationship, so too violence is destructive for everyone involved. This dialogue between fairness and care not only provides a better understanding of relations between the sexes but also gives rise to a more comprehensive portrayal of adult work and family relationships" (Gilligan, 1983:174).

As I have said the above material is drawn from scientific studies, and ones done mainly in First World societies at that. But it is corroborated by the exhaustive coverage by Ivan Illich, in his book *Gender* (1982), of societies and cultures as yet undeveloped by science and technology. All these are characterised by what he calls the "ambiguous complementarity" of genders. In all societies and cultures except (possibly) the European of the very recent past, men and women develop in asymmetrical ways, an asymmetry that is distinct from an inequality of power, and which is common to matriarchal as well as to patriarchal societies.

"Asymmetry is fundamental to the ambiguous complementarity of genders. It is constitutive of their very existence and determines their concrete relatedness" (1982:116). Given the assymetry that is present from the very start of the development of gender identity, the studies of Gilligan and others are a striking illustration of the complementarity of gender differences in the growth to moral maturity, and indeed in the whole process of personal growth and community as such.

Sexual life

We now come to consider sexual life in relation to gender. We will concentrate exclusively on sexual relations between people of different gender, but much of what we have to say about sex will be true of homosexual relationships as well.

It is not difficult to see the connection between the stories from the *Symposium* and the Bible about sex, and the theory of persons I have developed in this book. Persons, I have argued, depend on certain kinds of relations with other persons in order to develop as persons. And the underlying goal of this development, the "obscure object of desire" that motivates it, is to participate in a form of personal community that is characterised by complete mutuality and reciprocity. We desire to be part of this personal whole and in order to become capable of this we need to grow as persons by means of an influence that can only come to us from others. There is a clear parallel between our account of the desire for personal community and the accounts of sexual desire in the stories. How are they related?

Before one can answer this question one must be quite clear about the distinction between human sexual desire and the mating instinct present in all animal species. Human sexual desire is not directly related to fertility as such. This is revealed by its prodigality in all known cultures, however primitive: it is unrelated to the fertile period of women and continues during gestation. What then is it? What is sex all about?

My answer to this is that sex – sexual desire, sexual activity, sexual love – is the symbolic expression (and the most comprehensive symbolic expression) of the desire for personal growth and community and the interpersonal transactions that bring this about. It is symbolic because it is the expression of an essentially personal reality in a bodily way. We are bodily as well as personal beings.

That human sexuality is an essentially personal reality shows itself in the way that the definitive quality of sexual desire or pleasure, the sexiness of sex, derives from its intrinsic orientation to the other (Sartre, 1968; Nagel, 1979). Sexual activity and sensations wholly unrelated to other persons or to fantasies about persons or parts of persons, or fetishistic substitutes for other persons, lose their distinctively erotic tone.

The actual sexual quality resides not primarily in physical sensations but rather in the significance, the meaning, of the physical activity, its expressive and communicative value. The rhythm of mounting tension and release in sex would not only not produce powerful pleasure, it would be impossible, apart from the meaning given the activity by interpersonal interaction, imagined or real (Oraison, 1967).

Sexual activity is thus best understood as that bodily activity that is the full symbolic expression of our desire to realise ourselves as persons by participating in personal community with others. Because this desire is the most central and fundamental to our nature, sexual activity has a colossal range and power. It expresses both self-donation and receptivity, both ecstasy and potency, possession and surrender, opening up and taking in, the whole dialectic between self and other. Sexual activity differs from all other bodily activity because it expresses our awareness of our bodiliness itself, of our actually *being* a body.

The frequency of sex in human life is another sign of its symbolic character, its dependence on our drive to self-realisation for its power. Sex is repetitive because it is the image of a desire for community that is never completely fulfilled.

If I am right about the essentially symbolic character of sex then it follows that the relation between sexual development and personal development is an important one, as is that between sexual activity and the strictly personal qualities of the relationship in which it takes place. Because it is only symbolic of our deepest personal life, sexual development and maturity cannot be equated with personal growth and fulfilment. It is possible to be a wise and loving person and yet to have an undeveloped or even unintegrated sexuality.

Nevertheless the project of personal growth and community of gendered persons both requires the integration of sexual expression and personal development and provides our sexual life with a direction and a standard. Sexual interaction between people must be integrated into the strictly personal community between them and express it. To the extent to which they have developed as persons and really know and love each other for what they are, their sexual life will both reveal this character and also enhance and intensify it. Because sexual life is the expression of our awareness of our bodiliness as such, of our *being* a body – as distinct from, say, dancing, which is merely something we can do as a consequence of being a body – it is never neutral in respect of our growth as persons but is intrinsically expressive of it and a factor in it.

So the qualities of character and of interpersonal relationship that indicate personal growth and the achievement of personal community either do or do not find appropriate sexual expression. How best are we to conceive of what is or is not appropriate?

Good sex

We are considering the way in which our sexual life and activity can either be an impediment to our personal growth and the creation of community or promote it, and at the same time the way in which the degree to which we have or have not achieved these goals expresses itself sexually.

Bad sex is sex that fails to express the qualities that make for true personal community or is opposed to them. Sex can fail to do this in two different ways, either because it involves a withdrawal from the other, a kind of solitary sex, or because it involves a spurious intimacy with, typically, many others, promiscuity. The sexual life of gendered persons, because of the factors described above, is always directed towards an end that is intrinsic to it: sexual friendship. By sexual friendship I mean a relationship in which sexual activity becomes the expression of the personal growth and community of the persons involved.

In sexual friendship between persons of different gender, the intimate community between them makes possible for each the integration of the complementary aspects of the personal growth of persons of different gender noted above. Each realises their own humanity more fully, by making their own the complementary masculinity or femininity of the other.

C.S. Lewis has finely observed, in his *Four Loves* (1968), that erotic love is a face to face relationship whereas that of friendship is side by side. Friendship is always *about* something; the friends are united in something of common interest, something they both value. In the case of sexual friendship the common interest must be intrinsically related to sex. If, as I have argued sex is the bodily expression of our desire for (and hence the value of) personal community, then the appropriate object of sexual friendship must unite both these elements in a single project. This project will be the creation of personal community, not just between themselves – that is the proper goal of their erotic love (as distinct from their friendship) – but as such.

As such, personal community is not limited in any way to this or that group of persons, and so transcends the relationship the lovers have to one another. Thus the only adequate object of this interest is another person or persons. In a sexual relationship the proper object of this interest is the natural product of their bodily union, namely a child or children. Thus the procreation and education of other persons is a project arising naturally from the *personal* (and not simply the bodily) dimension of sexual friendship. This is so whether or not the couple have or can have children. Although the normal expression of this form of friendship is the procreation and education of their own children, it can be expressed in other ways, in adoption for instance, or in some of form of commitment to the personal growth of children (through welfare work or through one or other of the caring professions).

The above account of the intrinsic dynamism of human sexuality towards sexual friendship as I have defined it, implies its own ideal and criterion of success. Sexual friendship between persons of opposite gender finds its full expression in a deliberate permanent commitment to each other for the sake of personal community as such (entailing the possibility of children) that is publicly enacted. Each of these elements is essential; together they provide a definition of marriage that is intended to be normative for any of the many institutionalised forms that sexual union takes in various societies and cultures.

The different elements in marriage make possible different aspects of personal growth and community.

The commitment involved and its deliberate character are a very comprehensive exercise of one's capacity for self-affirmation and affirmation of another.

The permanence entailed expresses the virtually unconditional nature of the commitment. This is appropriate since the commitment to the personal community of marriage is a way of expressing one's commitment to the creation of personal community as such, and such a commitment can have no limit.

Such a commitment also makes psychologically possible a completeness of self-donation that would be impossible without it. And, as we all know, it takes more than a life-time to get to know another person properly.

The particularity of the relationship excludes polygamy. This is necessary to express the equal dignity of both partners and genders.

Public enactment expresses the non-exclusiveness of genuine personal community and the orientation of marriage to service of this end.

As we have said the intrinsic dynamism of sexual friendship has as its goal the creation of personal community in a bodily way. This is achieved in the procreation and education of a child, education being understood in a comprehensive sense, as its full integration into the personal community of the parents.

Family life

Parenthood is in fact the culmination of the development of gender identity in persons, and a final achievement of one's own gender identity for oneself, an achievement symbolised in the procreation of a child.

It is thus in parenthood that the differences between men and women are most fully revealed. Here the asymmetry is at its greatest; the complementarity is there but it has to be looked for. While she is pregnant the mother provides the medium through which the child relates to the world. She feeds and protects it, and provides every chemical it needs to grow from her own body. Her influence on it is not only physical; it is increasingly sensitive to her mental states. From the moment she knows that her desire to conceive has been fulfilled, a personal relationship between her and the child is set up that becomes increasingly mutual. The union between the mother and the child that is there from the beginning becomes increasingly personal. She is its home. It is the product and expression of her relationship with its father. In the full sexual friendship of marriage it is the focus of their friendship, what they most have in common, what their friendship is about.

So having the child inside her alters the mother's relation to the father. Insofar as they were equal origins of the child, she contains this relation within herself, embodied in its product. So her husband is inside her too. She has become his home as well. He, on the other hand, is also outside, separated from the child, and to that extent separated from the mother too, or from that in which their union is most fully realised. Pregnancy is something of a crisis for a father even when it is what he most desires. His function in pregnancy is to be the supportive milieu of the mother as she is for the child. In an ideal pregnancy the gender differences appear as an inward direction of interest and energy on the part of the mother and a correspondingly outward one on the part of the father. He must provide for her, make a home for her, give her peace for the child. This is both an economic and a political task, the origin of work and society.

Parents have equally important but complementary roles within the family. In the psychological development of the child the mother represents symbolically the home and the self, the father the world and the other. The integration of these complementary aspects by the child in its personal development, depends on their integration in the sexual relation between the parents. Other things being equal, the child needs the more or less constant presence of the mother during the first few years of its life; it also needs the regular attention of the father. Parent-child relations are in no sense property relations but are personal in the full sense, reciprocal and mutual, with equality of dignity and rights. The parent-child relation is productive of personal growth on both sides and thus involves "education" for both, in spite of the fact that education is the proper responsibility of the parent.

In one sense our account of personal growth and community in the sphere of gender is now complete. The development of one's gender identity in relation to persons of the opposite gender, and of one's own growth as a person in community with others, take place side by side. Each process is entwined with the other. Our account has however been an ideal account, distinguishing the essential elements in the process but without regard for the concrete circumstances in which it must take place.

Gender in society

But the sphere of gender is, of course, affected by all other spheres of human life. It is affected by the character of society as a whole, especially its economic and political aspects. If we are concerned with liberation in the sphere of gender, we shall have to take these aspects into account as well.

Society as a whole and all its institutions exist to serve personal growth and community. These are its fundamental and most important "product". This being the case, the gender-community of the family is the most important instrument by which this "work" is done: the procreation and education of persons and their integration into the personal community of others is the family's special function. Thus society exists to serve the family, and the family the person.

Government and the economy must reflect this; it must be facilitated by taxation and law. There could be, for instance, state grants for a certain number of children, and wages for the mother during the period of pregnancy and full-time child-care. Housework should be recognised as a necessary and demanding form of work. It should, moreover, be sufficiently remunerated from public funds, so that it becomes possible for a family to subsist in a simple but dignified life-style on just a single wage packet in addition to this. It should never be necessary for both parents to seek work *outside* the home in order to make a living.

As the basic agency of personal growth and the basic form of personal community, the family has duties as well as rights in respect of the wider society. In general it has a duty of hospitality and care for those outside it, especially the poor and needy. The traditional African idea of the extended family as something that includes far more than parents and children is perhaps the most common and most powerful institutional protection of the value of *ubuntu*. There ought to be some way of realising this in a setting created by European technology and development. In this way each family can be a *menage*, a cell in a local *domain* or neighbourhood, which is a truly personal and not just a geographical unit. The family in this sense is the natural personal environment for personal growth. The primary right and duty of education belongs to it and not to the state. A humane society will recognise and protect this right, and assist in the carrying out of this duty.

Equality and complementarity are the indexes of liberation in the sphere of gender. In the political realm this will mean that women play a part in society that is equal to that of men. It will also mean differential treatment in respect of different genders. No-one should be disadvantaged because of their gender; equity must prevail. Because of the complementarity of different genders, it is especially important that women and men be more or less numerically equally represented in government (both central and local), the police, education, welfare and health care services.

If liberation in the sphere of gender is to be achieved, equality and complementarity must be embodied in social institutions. The full range of the capacities of human nature is differently and incompletely expressed in either gender. So complementarity is both a natural fact and a personal and social goal. To take just one example that is big with social consequences:

women have a natural capacity for child-bearing and caring that men can never have. Her special creativity precisely as a woman is most fully expressed in bearing a child and in the personal relations that that entails. The evolutionary process that produced these capacities underlies the behavioural constants that appear in the most diverse cultures, as well as the self-understanding of the feminine that is transmitted by the various historical traditions of motherhood.

John Paul II emphasises the point I am making here when he writes, "There is no doubt that the equal dignity and responsibility of men and women fully justifies women's access to public functions. On the other hand the true advancement of women requires that clear recognition be given to the value of their maternal and family role, by comparison to all other public roles and other professions ... While it must be recognised that women have the same right as men to perform various public functions, society must be structured in such a way that wives and mothers are not in practice compelled to work outside the home, and that their families can live and prosper in a dignified way even when they themselves devote their full time to their own family. Furthermore, the mentality which honours women more for their work outside the home than for their work within the family must be overcome. This requires that men should truly esteem and love women with total respect for their personal dignity, and that society should create and develop conditions favouring work in the home" (1980:23–24).

The above is but one example of the way that liberation in the sphere of gender in a male-dominated society and culture such as ours requires the application of our principle of complementarity. The principle of equality is necessary but not sufficient on its own. To apply it in the abstract way characteristic of both liberalism and socialism is both to continue the subjection of women and to add to it by forcing on them the absolutised masculinity of modern European society and culture.

With this reflection we are brought face to face with the form taken by the human predicament in the sphere of gender in the contemporary world. It is one that is dramatically revealed in Africa, where developed and undeveloped societies and cultures exist side by side, and particularly in South Africa where apartheid has given this First World/Third World opposition such absolute stature and force.

The most obvious sign of the human predicament in the sphere of gender in the contemporary world is the immense inequality of economic and political power of women and men. In spite of the presence of equality at the heart of every contemporary political ideology, these inequalities remain, in both First and Third World societies. In the USA, as Illich points out, although all careers are now by law open to women, and 51% of women now work outside the home, as opposed to only 5% in 1880, the average earnings of women still stand to those of men in a ration of three to five (1982:24). In undeveloped countries the ratio is even worse.

There is however a difference between the inequalities of power in a developed society and an undeveloped one, such as the traditional patriarchal societies of Africa. In patriarchal societies there is a real complementarity of gender roles (Illich, 1982; Ruether, 1975). But such complementarity of power is non-homogeneous; each gender wields an entirely different but equally necessary range of powers, rather than more or less of the same kind of thing. As Illich puts it, "Asymmetry is fundamental to the ambiguous complementarity of genders. It is constitutive of their very existence and determines the character of their concrete relatedness. In contrast, power, which like a currency can circulate without respect to gender, ultimately tends towords symmetry. And while the asymmetry between genders has always inspired awe, the hierarchic distribution of power among theoretical equals inspires envy. For this reason I consider the genderless keyword *power* inadequate to express 1. either the mutual exclusion from their respective proper domains that is implicit in the concept of gender or 2. the relative dominance of male domains over that of females ..."(1982: 116).

By contrast in a scientifically and technologically developed society complementarity of gender domains and powers have been replaced by a homogeneous notion of power, both economic and political, as something that is equally wielded by all. Each worker, or voter, is treated as an abstractly equal unit of power, whether in a liberal capitalist or a socialist or communist society.

At the root of this change lie philosophical conceptions of humanity, either dualist or materialist. For the dualist men and women are equally persons because they have minds. Their bodies, and their gendered humanity, are forgotten. For the materialist bodily differences are merely biological; economics and politics and the power they involve are cultural arrangements that need have nothing to do with our (merely biological) nature.

The change from a traditional undeveloped society to a modern developed one affects women in a drastically different way from that in which it affects men. Starkly put, it is scientific and technological development itself that leads to the domination of society and culture by men and the qualities of their gender. Why this should be so I have not space to go into here. But all the authors I have consulted agree on this. It certainly seems to have something to do with the scientific and technological attitude to nature, including one's own nature, becoming dominant in society and culture. Because of this, humanity and the human milieu is increasingly separated from nature in an artificial environment. This separation affects women more immediately than men because of their natural capacity for child-bearing, but it results in a loss of their natural gender milieu for both genders, the resulting dominance of men notwithstanding. Liberation in the sphere of gender will thus mean the liberation of men as well as women even though it entails the loss of their present dominance.

The roots of gender conflict

Engels, in his *The Origins and History of the Family, Private Property and the State*, describes the oppression of women by men as the most fundamental form of human oppression. Insofar as this is true it would mean that liberation in the sphere of gender would entail liberation in all other spheres of human life as well. And this must be a reciprocal relation. Liberation in the sphere of work, for instance, is a necessary condition for liberation in the sphere of gender – and vice versa.

There is, it seems to me, nevertheless something fundamental about the conflict of genders that makes it a model for all other forms of opposition and oppression. However much society and culture changed there would still remain the likelihood of conflict and oppression between the genders. This is because, in a relationship between persons of different genders, unless each treats the other as a person, committed to knowing and loving them for their own sake, rather than purely on the basis of their gender identity, the possibility of true personal community – at whatever level of society – cannot be realised. For this reason, the problem of liberation in the sphere of gender is not just a scientific and technical problem. One is reminded once again of Gandhi's warning about dreaming of creating structures so perfect that no one will need to be good.

Sartre gives what is arguably the best philosophical account of the ultimate cause of conflict between people. And it bears out what I have said.

According to Sartre each of us is searching for an enduring identity, an absolute self-possession, that would combine the limitless freedom of consciousness with the determinate reality of an existing being. (Sartre calls this "being-in-itself-for-itself".) This we strive to achieve especially through our relationships with other people. The reason for this is as follows. For other people we exist as objectively real beings in the world, in a way that we cannot experience for ourselves; for ourselves we are always in a state of flux of self-creation. If however it were posssible to possess the other person, precisely as a free being for whom I am an objective being in the world, I would (through them) possess myself in this way as well.

Unfortunately the other person is involved in the same project; they want to possess me in order to achieve the kind of self-possession that I am striving for. They want to possess my freedom in order to gain the enduring reality that they appear to have for me. So Sartre writes, "While I attempt to free myself from the hold of the Other, the Other is trying to free himself from mine; while I seek to enslave the Other, the Other seeks to enslave me ... Conflict is the original meaning of being-for-others" (1968:340). For Sartre it is also the final meaning; the community of mutual recognition is intrinsically impossible because of the absolute nature of human freedom and its demands.

In Part Three of *Being and Nothingness* Sartre applies this account of the source of human conflict to sexual life. Here each person attempts to possess the other by means of the alternative strategies Sartre calls sadism and masochism. By sadism he means dominating the other so that they become merely a thing, a body, in your possession; by masochism he means making onself a mere thing, a body, in order to be possessed by the other.

A more concrete account of the fundamental sexual predicament could be given as follows: I so desire to be loved for myself, as the (free) person that I am that I do all in my power to make the other person love me in that way. They however are in a similar situation, a similar state of needing to be loved, and trying to extract love from me. The fact of the matter (as our account of the necessary conditions for personal growth in Chapter Seven tried to show) is that it is only when I am loved for my own sake that I am able to love the other person for theirs. And the same is true of them. So the battle for love proceeds, each needing to receive love in order to give it, each of us eternally master or slave, but never a genuinely loving couple.

That at any rate was Sartre's pessimistic conclusion. On our account of human freedom and the necessary conditions for personal growth and community it need not be so. One can nevertheless agree with Sartre that the sort of community we search for in sexual life, and whose absence so disrupts the whole sphere of gender relations, appears well-nigh impossible to achieve.

We have come to the end of our study of liberation in the sphere of gender. There are so many facets to this issue in this sphere that it was hardly possible even to touch on all of them. But I hope I have done enough, here and in the sphere of work in the previous chapter, to give some idea of how a philosophy of persons can be applied to particular spheres of life in the service of a comprehsive struggle for liberation.

I think that such a programme of applied philosophy is of great importance at the present time. As it is carried out it will supply a kind of "liberation map" by means of which one can relate the various suggestions for change to the overall aim of creating an environment for personal growth and community. But however thoroughly and perceptively such a programme was carried out, it would nevertheless still not be sufficient to effect a liberation process, to produce an actual "new South Africa". It is not enough to understand what is wrong, or even to know what to do to put it right. The real difficulty lies in the *doing* of it.

Chapter Thirteen

Religion: Power to Liberate

We must never lose sight of the fact that genuine human liberation does not consist merely in institutional changes, however radical these be. A change of institutions is necessary but it can never be sufficient. Genuine human liberation entails personal growth. And, as we have seen, this depends on certain kinds of personal transactions between persons. Such transactions can be helped (and certainly hindered) by the institutions in which people live. All human relations are after all mediated by the institutional milieu in which individuals live. But they can't be produced by them. Only a strictly personal energy elicited in a strictly personal way can do that.

So a crucially important question remains even after philosophy has done all it can to show us what we ought to do. It is a practical rather than a theoretical question: How can I do it? We need power as well as understanding. But a special kind of power, a strictly personal power that can only come to us from other persons who already have it, through personal community with them. And this indicates the problem: this kind of power can only come to me as a gift; I cannot produce it on my own. The sphere of human life that is concerned with this sort of power, the need for it, the understanding of it, the search for it and even, in the end (one hopes), the discovery and exercise of it, is that of religion.

I will conclude this application of philosophy to the problem of liberation with a brief account of the role that religion must play in the liberation struggle, in South Africa as in any other place.

The nature of religion

It must have struck the perceptive reader that in my discussion of liberation and of the different spheres of life in which philosophy can be applied to ensure the genuine humanity of the aims, means and conduct of the struggle for liberation, I made no mention of religion. I spoke of economic and family life, of the spheres of politics and welfare, and referred to those of education and law-enforcement as well. But religion was conspicuous by its absence.

This was not because I think that religion has no function in the liberation process, but because its function is unique. Religion is that human activity (understanding activity as including our cognitive, volitional and emotional powers) that has the fulfilment of the *whole* of our life, or our life *as a whole*, as its concern. As subjects we are able to envisage and be concerned with our life as a whole. In religion we do this in a distinctive way, as concerned with its fulfilment. The object of our religious activity is the fulfilment of the *whole* of life, of all our needs, especially the most fundamental, in a complete and final way. All religions worthy of the name are concerned with this, whatever name they give to their ultimate goal – salvation, enlightenment, nirvana, satori or no name at all. And all religions see their gods as sources of power sufficient to achieve this goal. Finally, all religions see this goal as transcending human powers to achieve. In this sense the gods are always seen as transcendent beings (Kung, 1990; Rahner, 1968, 1969, 1978; Shutte, 1976).

In spite of having this distinctive character of being concerned with and having to deal with the *whole* of life, religion is always also a *particular* human activity, embodying particular practices, existing in particular institutional forms. In fact this is precisely the peculiarity of religion: it is a particular activity that has as its proper object the whole of life. For this reason it has *no* special sphere, whether that of family, education, politics or whatever. And this is what gives it its essentially symbolic, or sacramental, nature. It is a particular activity that stands for and expresses a concern with the whole of life. Hence specifically religious acts, such as prayer and worship, though directly concerned with human fulfilment, are not pragmatic in any ordinary sense. They do not get things done, or take the place of ordinary moral and political activity. They are, rather, simply expressive. They are expressive of the meaning of human life for the worshippers, of what they suffer, what they hope for, and of the character of the power that can bring them to fulfilment.

From what I have said it will be apparent that all religions see human life as involving a predicament which human power is in principle unable to overcome. But each particular religion has its own particular idea of what the predicament is. And any particular conception of the human predicament can be inadequate or mistaken. Indeed the modern phenomenon of secularisation derives its momentum from the increased power of humanity to meet needs that were once thought to be quite beyond human power and solely in the gift of the gods. In the light of the development of modern science and technology, even death could perhaps now be seen, at least in principle, as being within human power to overcome – in the sense of being put off indefinitely, for a privileged few.

The philosophical conception of persons developed in this book does however identify a natural (and therefore universal) need of each of us that we are unable of our own power to fulfil. That is the need to grow as a person and the desire for personal community. Such a need does indeed transcend our own powers, in the sense that we require the kind of initiative and influence of another person which essentially transcends our control, if it is to be met. To develop as a person we stand in need of a strictly personal power which, if it is to be acquired by us at all, has to be given us by another.

If our account of the necessary conditions of personal growth is accurate then it does indeed identify a power that transcends our own but which we need in order to develop the capacity and satisfy the desire that is quite fundamental to our nature as persons, namely the desire for personal community with others. It therefore supplies us with a criterion for judging religions. Whatever else a religion offers, to be worthy of our allegiance it must offer to supply this sort of power. And if human liberation depends on personal growth in individuals, then it is only a religion that meets this need that will have a part to play in the liberation struggle.

The function of religion in a liberation struggle

From the point of view developed in this book religion has an irreplaceable role to play in the liberation struggle. This is that it bring into being in the lives of persons that distinctive personal power productive of personal growth and community. It is concerned to produce personal growth and community in every sphere of life, and so too with the creation of institutions that foster rather than impede this growth. It exhibits two characteristic ways of achieving this end, one negative, one positive.

The negative way is the transformation of an inhuman and dehumanising situation through a critique of the ideologies and power structures that embody the idolatrous attempts at self-realisation of various groups, in the manner we have described. Religion is concerned with the "spirit" of our life in each dimension of society, and especially to prevent our developing absolute and unconditional attachments to particular ideas and groups, and so becoming enslaved by them.

In this critical opposition to every inauthentic attempt at self-realisation in every sphere of life, religion inevitably puts itself outside society as the peculiar (prophetic) institution that is concerned with the reformation of society as a whole. Of course any particular religion is not really "outside" society. It exists as one institution among others. But it has, as I have already said, a unique character. And it is in this that its positive function in the bringing into being of personal growth and community consists.

The positive function of religion in the liberation struggle derives from the symbolic or sacramental character of religious activity and institutions. As I have said, this symbolic character derives from the fact that religious institutions are particular institutions that are concerned with the character of the whole of human life and society. Religious activity is a particular kind of activity whose purpose is to express and enact our concern with the whole of life and its fulfilment. Hence the peculiar, non-pragmatic, dramatic, "make-believe" character of religious activity and institutions.

If we take the activity of liturgy (or prayer or worship) as the typical religious activity, this symbolic character is easy to discern. In the Christian eucharist, for example, the community of believers enacts in a symbolic way (by participating in a fellowship meal) the communion with Jesus (and so with each other and with God) they believe has been made possible by his death and resurrection. It does this by expressing this faith in a dramatic way by words and gesture, and so creating an appropriate symbolic form, through which the actual interpersonal power that is capable of bringing about what is hoped for, can be exercised.

The power to achieve personal growth is not a power that can be self-generated. It comes to each of us from others. Religious institutions and activities create the setting in which this can really happen. The setting, essentially symbolic, refers to the whole of life and to each sphere of it. It is there, in real as distinct from symbolic life, that personal growth occurs (or doesn't). But it does so by virtue of the meaning expressed in the religion, and the personal power enacted through it.

A question remains, of course, as to whether religion – or a particular religion, or any particular religion – really "works". This question has no theoretical answer. The only relevant answer is in the life of the believer.

Does it or does it not reveal the power to produce personal growth and community? This question is related to the further philosophical question regarding the ultimate source of the power capable of producing personal growth and community. Such power might transcend the powers of the individual, but does it transcend human power as such?

Our account of the necessary conditions of personal growth might be understood to have already supplied a negative answer to this question. But it was not intended to. Our account, though borrowing from the concrete details of human life, was intended to be abstract and ideal. We worked out the necessary conditions; we did not make any claims about their occurrence. And on the account of the necessary conditions which we gave, there does remain a problem about the ultimate cause of personal growth.

Since persons are persons only by virtue of a capacity for free activity, how is it possible for *any* external influence to do anything but inhibit this capacity's development? It may be the case that this is possible only on the supposition of the existence and causal influence of a strictly transcendent being whose activity would be simply incommensurable with that of any finite being – as for instance is the case with the Christian conception of God as our creator and saviour.

For a detailed discussion of human freedom as evidence for the existence of God, I would refer the reader to my two articles in *Modern Theology* (1984:67–79; 1987:157–177).

Hans Kung, in his recent *Global Responsibility* (1990) – which is subtitled "In search of a new world ethic", argues that there can be no world peace without peace between the world's religions. This is because world peace depends in the last resort on the absolute or unconditional acceptance of, and commitment to, the value of human persons and their fulfilment (what Kung calls the *humanum*), and only religion can supply this essential note of the unconditional or absolute. "Let us be quite clear: even those who have no religion can also lead a life which is authentically human and in this sense moral: this is the expression of human autonomy within the world. But there is one thing that those who have no religion cannot do, even if in fact they want to accept unconditional norms for themselves: they cannot give a reason for the absoluteness and universality of ethical obligation ... No, the categorical quality of ethical demand, the unconditioned nature of the ought, cannot be grounded by human beings, who are conditioned in many ways, but only by that which is unconditional: by an Absolute which can provide an over-arching meaning and which embraces and permeates individual human nature and indeed the whole of human society" (1990:51–53).

It is clear from this that Kung sees an essential function for religion in the struggle for human liberation wherever it occurs. Nor is its function merely that of providing a theoretical foundation for commitment to the struggle. "For religions have means of shaping the whole of human existence, not just for an intellectual elite but also for broad strata of the population – means which have been tested by history, adapted to cultures and made specific for the individual. Religion certainly cannot do everything, but it can disclose a certain 'more' in human life and bestow it ... Through common symbols, rituals, experiences and goals, religion can create a sense of feeling at home, a sense of trust, faith, certainty, strength for the self, security and hope: a spiritual community and allegiance" (1990:54). This is another way of making the same point as I have made: that religion supplies *power*.

South Africa and secularisation

In a South African context there can be no doubt that religion is an extremely important factor in the liberation struggle. Certainly insofar as apartheid has been an element in the South African predicament, religion has both provided its ultimate justification and support, and fought against it as heretical and demonic.

From our point of view however the religious situation in South Africa must be understood in terms of the phenomenon of secularisation that dominates the religious scene in First World countries. Compared with such countries South African society is only very partially and unevenly secularised. Religion still plays a large role in public life. Nevertheless secularisation is here to stay – in just the same way as European scientific and technological culture is. So if the character and strength of our religious life is of crucial importance to the liberation struggle, we must find a way of being religious in a secular world.

The essence of secularisation consists in its connection with science and technology. It comprises two components. In a sacral world-view, say that of pre-renaissance Europe, reality is thought to consist of two radically distinct "worlds", a supernatural one and a natural one. Folk-religion at any rate locates the abode of the gods in a supernatural realm, while that of humanity is the world of nature. The supernatural is just as real as the natural, if not more so, in the sacral consciousness. In fact it determines what happens in the natural world, human lives included. The development of modern science changed all this. There was only really one world, the world studied by science. The supernatural became only a shadowy reality, if real at all, and ceased to play a dominant part in human life.

That is the first (theoretical) component of secularisation: the change from two worlds to one. The second (and more practical) component is related to it. In the sacral world-view it was the supernatural forces that were in ultimate control of nature and human life. In a secular world-view it is humanity itself, through the technology that science has made possible. So secularisation means that there is only one world, the world revealed by science, and that in this world humanity is able to exercise control, the control provided by technology of various kinds.

In South Africa different religious bodies are secularised to different degrees. Understandably in the beginning, in Europe, secularisation was seen as the enemy of religion. However, over time Christianity, and to an extent Judaism, came to grips with it and adapted the understanding and practice of the faith to the new view of the world. As I shall presently indicate, secularisation is not simply incompatible with religion; a religious view of the world is not necessarily a sacral one.

In South Africa certain forms of Judaism and certain Christian churches have assimilated secularisation the most thoroughly. Fundamentalist Christian sects oppose it strongly, as do most forms of Islam. The so-called African independent churches, religious bodies combining Biblical as well as traditional African elements, are hardly secularised at all. And African traditional religion is still completely sacral.

The significance of secularisation for understanding the role of religion in the liberation struggle must now be spelt out. A central aspect (some would say *the* central aspect) of the secular view of the world is the idea of human freedom. Indeed the whole modern focus on the idea of liberation derives from the secularisation process. A particular understanding of human freedom is central to the view of persons developed in this book. If this view is right, religion must fit in with it, if it is to have a positive influence in the struggle for liberation. Forms of religion that have not come to terms with secularisation but are still wedded to a sacral view of the world, will tend to be irreconcilable with human freedom. They have still to pass through the "brook of fire" (Feuer – bach) Marx spoke of.

At this point it is perhaps necessary to explain why religion as such is not necessarily incompatible with secularisation. In particular a Thomist understanding of God and God's relationship with the universe is unaffected by a secular view of the world. There are also aspects of a traditional African understanding of God that make for an integration into a secular world-view. As yet this has not been done. But, in the spirit of the present project, I do not see why it could not be. And I think that Thomist philosophy might well be the best fitted for the attempt.

The Thomist understanding of God in relation to the universe can be indicated by the linked notions of transcendence and immanence and the concept of incommensurability. These terms define, in a philosophical way, the traditional Christian notion of creation.

To say that God is the creator of the universe should not be understood as implying that God made the universe as a watchmaker might make a watch, which then has the capacity to continue on its own independent of its maker. Creation should not be tied simply to the beginning of everything in this way, especially as it suggests a kind of ensuing independence of the universe of God's creative activity. A better model would be that of a singer singing a song. At each moment of its existence the song is dependent on the singer for all that it is. The same is true of the relationship of creation: the universe is wholly dependent on God's creative activity for all that it is and does at each moment of its existence. To say that God is transcendent is to say that God is not the universe that he creates, nor any part of it; to say that God is immanent is to say that God is "in" the universe and every part and event of it, as the cause of its existence at each moment that it exists. Taken together the notions of transcendence and immanence entail God's incommensurability with creation or any created thing. One cannot add God and the universe and make two.

Perhaps this needs further explanation. One can add one apple and another apple and make two apples because they are both apples. One can even add an orange and an apple and get two fruit, because they are both fruit. In general one can add anything in the universe to anything else and get two things. There is some common measure, some reciprocal relation. In the case of God and the universe there is not – no common measure, no reciprocal relation. One can clarify what is being said here by means of an example.

My daughter, aged six, once asked me, "Where's God?" Luckily for me she was, at the time, seated at a table drawing a picture of a little girl in a garden. I pointed at the picture and asked her, "Where're you in the picture?" "I'm not in the picture; I'm drawing it", she answered. So I was able to say, "Well, God is not anywhere in the world; he's making it." And she understood. This exemplifies our present point insofar as my daughter and the little girl in the picture can be seen as incommensurable. There were not two little girls in the room. Nor were there even (in a certain sense) two things, since the reality of a drawn image is of such a different kind from that of a living person. The same is true of Aquinas' understanding of God and the universe and the relation between them, the relationship of creation which is a one-way relation of dependence of the universe on God for everything that it is and does.

This understanding of the relation between God and the universe might seem adequate for everything except for persons, since they are free. In fact it holds for them as well. To say that persons are free means that they are free from total determination by other causes *within* the universe. The only way persons could be free of *God* would be by not existing. And to think that they depended on God for their initial creation and then existed with a certain independence of his influence, would be to make God finite and part of the universe and therefore unable to be a creator in the strict sense at all.

The notion of incommensurability saves us from this muddle. God's power is not something that could be either added to or subtracted from our power. It is not the case that either God has done the deed or I have. The more the action is God's the more it is my own. In fact God influences me in two ways. He influences me through the ordinary operation of natural and social forces on me. And to that extent I am not free. And he influences me directly, through my own mind and will. And this is what makes me free of all other causes of an external type.

For a fuller discussion of the notion of incommensurability in Thomist philosophy of religion I refer the reader to Herbert McCabe's *God Matters* (1987), especially the first three chapters.

With such an understanding of God as creator, the duality of the sacral world-view simply vanishes, as does the opposition between God's activity and our own. God is by no means the enemy of human freedom, but rather its necessary support. In fact I think the Thomist view of persons as I have developed it in the present work can go even further than this in providing us with a positive model of God's creation of free beings and their free acts.

Consider our account of the necessary conditions for personal growth, the mother-child model for instance. The more the mother influences the child in a strictly personal way, the more the child's capacity for self-determination is developed. Can one not take this interpersonal transaction as the true model for God's causality as our creator. God is like our mother only more so. Whereas her influence causes the child's capacity for self-determination to grow, God's influence causes the capacity itself. And, of course, it is also God's (incommensurable) influence *within* the influence of the mother that makes the paradoxical production and growth of our freedom possible at all. But that is a topic that goes beyond the scope of this discussion.

Religion and freedom

Thus we see that religion is by no means necessarily incompatible with human freedom. Hence it is clear that religion can have a positive function in the liberation process, of the kind that I have described above. Traditional African conceptions of God tend to stress God's immanence in all worldly causality, especially that involved in relations between persons. The reader should refer back to our discussion of *seriti* in Chapter Five, and also to the work of Setiloane (1986) and Tempels (1959) on this topic. If it is possible, as I hope to have shown, to integrate in a philosophical treatment the African emphasis on the dependence of persons on other persons for their development as persons, and the Thomist notion of the freedom and subjectivity of persons, then I see no reason why a Thomist philosophy of religion should not do the same for traditional African religion.

At all events the sort of synthesis of European and African ideas that I have attempted, using contemporary Thomist philosophy for the purpose, could provide the basis for dialogue between the different religious traditions in South Africa. Such dialogue could prove useful as they try to come to terms with secularisation. But it is essential if religion is to be able to play its proper role in the liberation struggle, which is to empower persons to develop as persons and to realise personal community in every sphere of South African life.

Kung would agree with what I have argued here. He in fact uses his notion of the *humanum* in just this way: "a religion is true and good to the degree that it serves humanity, to the degree that in its doctrine of faith and morals, its rites and institutions, it advances men and women in their identity, sense of meaning and sense of dignity, and allows them to attain to a meaningful and fruitful existence" (1990:90).

So for Kung, as for us, an understanding of the place of religion in human life, that both recognises and vindicates human freedom, is necessary if human liberation or peace is to be authentically aimed at. "True humanity is the presupposition for true religion. That means that the *humanum* (respect for human dignity and basic values) is a minimal requirement of any religion: where authentic religious feeling is to be realised, there must at least be humanity (that is a minimal criterion). But in that case why religion?

True religion is the fulfilment of true humanity. That means that religion (as the expression of all-embracing meaning, supreme values, unconditional obligation) is an optimal presupposition for the realisation of the *humanum*: there must be religion, in particular (that is the maximal criterion) where humanity is to be realised and made concrete as a truly unconditioned and universal obligation" (1990:91).

A philosophical conception of humanity, such as we have been trying to establish, has an important role to play in this connection, and nowhere more so than in Africa.

Bibliography

Apostel, L. 1981. *African Philosophy: Myth or Reality*. Gent: E. Story - Scientia.
Bodunrin, P. 1981. 'The Question of African Philosophy'. *Philosophy* 56: 161-179.
Buber, M. 1958. *I and Thou*, tr.R.G. Smith. London: Clark.
Buber, M. 1961. *What is Man*. London: Fontana.
Busia, A. 1967. *Africa in Search of Democracy*. London: Collins.
Cirne-Lima, C. *Personal Faith*. New York: Herder.
Donceel, J. 1967. *Philosophical Anthropology*. New York: Sheed and Ward.
Engels, F. 1963. *The Origins and History of the Family, Private Property and the State*. New York: International.
Farrer, A. 1979. *Finite and Infinite*. New York: Seaburg.
Feldstein, L. 1976. 'Personal Freedom: The Dialectics of Self-Possession'. pp61-85 in R. Johann (ed.), *Freedom and Value*. New York: Fordham.
Fromm, E. 1961. *Marx's Concept of Man*. New York: Ungar.
Gilleman, G. 1959. *The Primacy of Charity in Moral Theology*. New York: Newman.
Gilligan, C. 1981. 'Moral Development in the College Years' in A. Chickering (ed.), *The Modern American College*. San Franscisco: Jossey-Bass.
Gilligan, C. 1983. *In a Different Voice*. Cambridge: Harvard.
Gilligan, C. and Murphy J.M. 1979. 'Development from Adolescence to Adulthood' in D. Kuhn (ed.), *Intellectual Development Beyond Childhood*. San Francisco: Jossey-Bass.
Gyekye, K. 1987. *An Essay on African Philosophical Thought*. London: Cambridge.
Hegel, G. (1807) 1910. *The Phenomenology of Mind*, tr J.B. Baillie. London: Allen and Unwin.
Heidegger, M. 1962. *Being and Time*, tr. J. Macquarrie and E. Robinson. London: S.C.M.
Heron, J. 1970. 'The Phenomenology of Social Encounter: The Gaze'. *Philosophy and Phenomenological Research* 10. pp243-264.
Hill, E. 1984. *Being Human*. London: Geoffrey Chapman.
Illich, I. 1982. *Gender*. New York: Pantheon.
Johann, R. 1966. *The Meaning of Love*. New York: Paulist.
Johann, R. 1975. 'Person, Community and Moral Commitment'. pp155-175 in R.J. Roth (ed.), *Person and Community*. New York: Fordham.
Johann, R. 1976. 'Freedom and Morality from the Standpoint of Communication'. pp45-59 in R. Johann (ed.), *Freedom and Value*. New York: Fordham.
John Paul II, 1980. *Familiaris Consortio*.
John Paul II, 1981. *Laborem Exercens*.
John Paul II, 1991. *Centesimus Annus*.
Kellog, W. and Kellog, L. 1933. *The Ape and the Child*. New York: McGraw-Hill.

Kung, H. 1990. *Global Responsibility*. London: SCM.

Langer, S. 1971. *Philosophy in a New Key*. Cambridge: Harvard.

Lawrence, D.H. 1931. *Apropos of Lady Chatterley's Lover*. London: Penguin.

Leo XIII, 1891. *Rerum Novarum*.

Lewis, C.S. 1968. *The Four Loves*. London: Collins.

Lonergan, B. 1957. *Insight*. New York: Philosophical Library.

Luijpen, W. 1960. *Existential Phenomenology*. Pittsburgh: Duquesne.

MacMurray, J. 1957. *The Self as Agent*. London: Faber.

Macmurray, J. 1959. *Persons in Relation*. London: Faber.

May, R. 1980. *Sex and Fantasy*. New York: W W Norton.

McCabe, H. 1987. *God Matters*. London: Geoffrey Chapman.

Mead, M. 1950. *Male and Female*. London: Penguin.

Menkiti, I. A. 1979. 'Person and Community in African Traditional Thought'. pp157-168 in R.A. Wright (ed.), *African Philosophy*. New York: University Press of America.

Merleau-Ponty, M. 1964. 'The Child's Relation with Others' in J.M. Edie (ed.), *The Primacy of Perception*. Evanston: North-Western.

Moir, A. and Jessel, D. 1989. *Brain Sex*. London: Joseph.

Mulago, V. 1971. 'Vital Participation' in Dickson and Ellinworth (eds.), *Biblical Revelation and African Beliefs*. London: Butterworth.

Nagel, T. 1979. *Mortal Questions*, London: Cambridge.

Nédoncelle, M. 1966. *Love and the Person*, tr. Sr. Ruth Adelaide S.C., New York: Sheed and Ward.

Nolan, A. 1982. 'The Political and Social Context' in A.Prior (ed.), *Catholics in Apartheid Society*. Cape Town: David Philip.

Nolan, A. 1989. *God in South Africa*. Cape Town: David Philip.

Oraison, M. 1967. *The Human Mystery of Sexuality*. New York: Sheed and Ward.

Oruka, H.O. 1978. 'Four Trends in Current African Philosophy'. William Amo Symposium: Accra.

Pius XI, 1931. *Quadragesimo Anno*.

Plato, 1951. *The Symposium*. London: Penguin.

Rahner, K. 1965. *Hominisation*. London: Burns and Gates.

Rahner, K. 1968. *Spirit in the World*. London: Herder.

Rahner, K. 1969. *Hearers of the Word*. London: Sheed and Word.

Rahner, K. 1978. *Foundations of Christian Faith*. London: Dartan, Longman and Todd.

Ruch, E. and Anyanwu, K. 1984. *African Philosophy*. Rome: Catholic Book Agency.

Ruether, R. 1975. *New Woman, New Earth*. New York: Seabury.

Sartre, J-P. 1968. *Being and Nothingness*. New York: Citadel.

Scheler, M. 1973. *Formalism in Ethics and Non-Formal Ethics of Values*, tr. M. Frings. (1916). Evanston: North-Western.

Schumacher, E.F. 1973. *Small is Beautiful*. London: Abacus.

Schumacher, E.F. 1980. *Good Work*. London: Abacus.

Senghor, L. 1939. *L'Homme de Couleur Symposium*. Paris.

Senghor, L. 1963. 'Negritude and African Socialism' in K. Kirkwood (ed.), *St. Anthony's Papers* No. 15. Oxford.

Senghor, L. 1965. *On African Socialism*. Stanford.
Senghor, L. 1966. 'Negritude'. *Optima* 16. 1-8.
Setiloane, 1986. *African Theology*. Johannesburg: Skotaville.
Shutte, A. 1976. 'A Theory of Religion'. *International Philosophical Quarterly* 16: 289 - 300.
Shutte, A. 1984. 'What makes us Persons'. *Modern Theology* Vol. 1. pp67-79.
Shutte, A. 1987. 'A New Argument for the Existence of God'. *Modern Theology* Vol. 3. pp157-177.
Strasser, S. 1969. *The Idea of Dialogal Phenomenology*. Pittsburgh: Duquesne.
Tallon, A. 1982. *Personal Becoming*. Marquette University Press: Milwaukee.
Taylor, C. 1975. *Hegel*. London: Cambridge.
Taylor, J.V. 1963. *The Primal Vision*. London: S.C.M.
Teilhard de Chardin, P. 1959. *The Phenomenon of Man*. London: Collins.
Tempels, P. 1959. *Bantu Philosophy*. Paris: Presence Africaine.
Tevoedjre, A. 1979. *Poverty. The Wealth of Mankind*. London: Oxford.
Toner, J. 1968. *The Experience of Love*. Washington: Corpus.
Tucker, R. 1967. *Philosophy and Myth in Karl Marx*. London: Cambridge.
Ver Eecke, W. 1975. 'The Look, The Body and The Other'. pp224-246 in D. Ihde (ed.), *Dialogues in Phenomenology*. The Hague: Nijhoff.
Weil, S. 1952. *The Need For Roots*. London: Routledge and Kegan Paul.
Weil, S. 1958. *Oppression and Liberty*. London: Ark.
Wiredu, K. 1980. *Philosophy and an African Culture*. London: Cambridge.
Wiredu, K. 1977. 'Philosophy and Our Culture'. *Proceedings of the Ghana Academy of Arts and Sciences*.

Index